SYSTEMIC COUPLE THERAPY
AND DEPRESSION

Other titles in the
Systemic Thinking and Practice Series
edited by David Campbell & Ros Draper
published and distributed by Karnac Books

Credit Card orders, Tel: 020-7584-3303; Fax: 020-7823-7743; Email: books@karnacbooks.com

SYSTEMIC COUPLE THERAPY AND DEPRESSION

Elsa Jones and Eia Asen

Foreword by
Gianfranco Cecchin

Introduction by
Julian Leff

Systemic Thinking and Practice Series

Series Editors
David Campbell & Ros Draper

London & New York
KARNAC BOOKS

First published in 2000 by
H. Karnac (Books) Ltd., 58 Gloucester Road, London SW7 4QY

A subsidiary of Other Press LLC, New York

British Library Cataloguing in Publication Data

A C.I.P. for this book is available from the British Library

   ISBN 1 85575 221 2

10 9 8 7 6 5 4 3 2 1

Edited, designed, and produced by Communication Crafts

Printed in Great Britain by Polestar AUP Aberdeen Limited

www.karnacbooks.com

ACKNOWLEDGEMENT

We would like to thank Julian Leff and his team at the Institute of Psychiatry, London, for deciding to turn their research lens onto systemic therapy and for carrying out their work to the highest scientific standard. We have found their encouragement very supportive.

CONTENTS

EDITORS' FOREWORD

The excitement surrounding the publication of this book stems from the fact that it is based upon a recent research project that demonstrated the effectiveness of systemic therapy. The news of Elsa Jones and Eia Asen's project and the subsequent results were greeted with great enthusiasm in the systemic/family therapy field. Their work was bold, innovative, and vital. When we heard the results of the study, many of us were asking the authors, "How did you do it?"—and this book is their reply to that question.

The book is about the couple therapy itself, how it was conceptualized, and how it was carried out, and it is written with therapists in mind. Jones and Asen have made their approach to marital therapy accessible to practitioners by describing the variety of techniques they used in their work, and by analysing several cases in great detail to highlight the process of their therapy. But even though the therapy was conducted within the framework of a manual, there is a surprising amount of variation in the approaches used by the authors, and this culminates in an illuminating dialogue at the end of the book in which these differences are explored fully.

As Editors, it is a pleasure to bring into the series a book that so clearly unites the researcher's rigorous pursuit of understanding with the therapist's desire to help people change. Many therapists work in the public sector where the paymaster is increasingly asking for the evidence to prove that therapy is worth paying for. This is a question that must be answered if the systemic therapies are to have a future within the public services, and this book is one voice that answers the query but also provides therapists with a detailed presentation of ways to work effectively with couples.

David Campbell
Ros Draper
London
June 2000

FOREWORD

Gianfranco Cecchin

This book created by Elsa Jones and Eia Asen provides many opportunities for a systemic therapist to reflect about many issues that are usually sources for discussions and controversy. One important question that must be considered is how many restrictions a systemic therapist can tolerate, since he or she is usually accused of:

1. not having a clear plan of therapy and not being goal-oriented;
2. not needing to have a precise diagnosis to be able to function;
3. taking, more often than not, a position of neutrality—that is, having a low level of indignation in the face of the terrible things humans do to each other;
4. not being strategic—that is, not having a clear intentionality.

Instead, in this research project we can appreciate the great value there is in creating artificial restrictions that have the paradoxical effect of giving great freedom to the therapists involved.

The boundaries are created by an independent agency—the team of researchers. These boundaries permit the following:

- A diagnosis is made by the psychiatric authorities
- There is a setting (psychiatric hospital or clinic) defined by the agency
- There is a goal, the specific goal of the research project, under- standable by everyone involved—namely, can a partner be of help to someone who suffers from a very common, well-known devastating illness: depression?

The need to follow research criteria as precise as possible also offers the opportunity to invent precise rules. One such rule, for example, is: the number of sessions is regulated not by the need of each client but by the requirements of the research project. The same goes for the length of therapy (9 months) and the flexibility of the participation in the project (e.g. how many times people can attend as a couple or alone).

Within all these artificial limits imposed by the research model, Eia and Elsa act with great freedom and creativity, as demon- strated in this beautiful book. The two authors, with their clearly different styles, prejudices, and attitudes handle themselves with ease within the mysteries, the contradictions, and the unpredict- ability of the stories brought to them by the so-called "patients"— stories that either are tragic or comic or are tragic and comic at the same time.

The results of the research are not the responsibility of the therapists: it is the job of the researchers to study the results, and they have no other goal than to find out if this type of therapy works with depressed persons. The therapists themselves are not committed to demonstrate anything. The impression they give is that they would behave in the same way in another context. I risk the hypothesis that Elsa and Eia would not have changed their behaviour even if they had found out that the results of the re- search were not as positive as in reality they turned out to be.

Another interesting constraint dictated by the research model is that this so-called systemic therapy ought to be recognized by an independent observer. By viewing videotaped sessions, Professor

Leff's team was, in fact, able to recognize Eia and Elsa's style as being distinctly different from the style observed in sessions conducted by a cognitive or a drug therapist. Even if Elsa and Eia are quite different from each other, there must still be some principles that both of them follow in a natural way. I dare suggest that these principles are the classical ones: belief that the world we see is a world of communication, that people exist, play, and suffer in relation to someone, and that the job of the therapist is to be curious and fascinated by the struggles of his or her clients without inducing a wish necessarily to change them.

Within these premises, we can see how each of the styles of the authors becomes very coherent: the fast and ironic style of Eia, or the participation in human suffering of Elsa. Elsa's indignation in the face of violence, abuse, and poverty comes through very clearly and very consistently within these premises. For me, all this demonstrates that someone can be totally free to use his or her own style without giving up the basic principles of systemic thinking.

The problem we often have—namely, of how important it is, to be able to work, to have a diagnosis—is resolved here in a very brilliant way. Systemic therapists have always had the doubt—or the conviction—that the act of labelling a person with a diagnosis contributes to the problems that the person has. Sometimes, the diagnosis is as responsible for initiating a person into the career of the chronic deviant, the mental patient, the criminal, and so forth. In this book, we do not see any attempt to take away the diagnosis from people, a diagnosis that sometimes has been with them for years. In one case described here, the diagnosis becomes a member of the family and is accepted as a long-term and indispensable companion in life.

This research is perhaps demonstrating the strange fact that therapies done under some form of strong constraints (court-mandated cases, consultations with prisoners, or therapies done in mental hospitals) sometimes produce better results than therapies done under more "collaborative" circumstances. It could also be that the therapist is constrained if not constricted by many rules, some of which may even be liberating—for example, the rule that the therapist is not obliged to succeed in curing people. In this book, the only obligation of the therapists is to complete the research, even in uncomfortable and discouraging contexts (as described by Elsa).

This book can, I believe, be a stimulus to initiate similar research projects in similar situations in the vast field of mental health care in public services, and the authors are to be congratulated for writing it.

INTRODUCTION

Julian Leff

Working with families in an attempt to produce change is a highly informative way of learning about family systems and how they function. In this sense, the therapist acts as a probe into the system. Unlike a thermometer, another kind of probe, the therapist acts on the family as well as being acted upon by them. Sensitive therapists record both their effect on the family and the family's effect on them and utilize these data to shape their interventions. It is rare, however, for therapists to write down their accumulated experience in a systematized form to act as a guide for others to follow. The general reluctance to commit their expertise to paper must stem partly from therapists' belief in the unique quality of their personal style, which is not transmissible. In the 1970s, when my colleagues and I began to work, in the context of a randomized trial, with families with a schizophrenic member, we did not start by writing a manual. This was not attributable to elitist attitudes, but was due to the fact that we were feeling our way in uncharted territory. Only after we had modified our original intervention through trial and error over fifteen years did we feel confident enough to publish a manual (Kuipers, Leff, & Lam, 1992).

Our manual became the basis for a training course in schizophrenia family work, which is now one of the main modules in the Thorn Initiative. The impetus to develop a training programme came from a sharp awareness of the thousands of families in the United Kingdom who were looking after relatives with schizophrenia, without appropriate help from professionals. But before establishing the training, it was necessary to demonstrate that the intervention was efficacious. The evidence came not only from two controlled trials that we ourselves conducted, but from similar research carried out by teams in the United States, the United Kingdom, and China. The sequence of stages in the research is worth spelling out, since its success in relation to schizophrenia has persuaded us to follow the same programme with respect to depression.

The first stage is to establish a relationship between relatives' emotional attitudes, measured as Expressed Emotion (EE), and the course of the psychiatric condition. It is likely to require a series of studies with consistent results to provide sufficient evidence for this. The next step is to design an intervention aimed at rnodifying the relationship between the carers and the patient. If this is successful, the necessary skills have to be identified and disseminated to the appropriate professionals through training programmes. Once the relationship between relatives' EE and the course of depression had been established, we were ready to advance to the second stage of designing and testing an intervention. We considered that the necessary expertise to achieve this already existed in the form of systemic therapy, so we approached two of the most highly regarded exponents of this approach in the United Kingdom, the authors of this book. We had learned from our research on schizophrenia that it was preferable to start with a manual rather than to finish with one, so we persuaded Eia and Elsa to undertake this daunting task. Their attempts to meet our demands are documented in chapters one and two.

This manual has two main purposes. First, it can act as the basis of a training programme in systemic couple therapy, which we see as the next phase of the work on depression. It is also explicit about the range of techniques used and can therefore inform the next generation of research studies, which should have the aim of identifying in this therapy the essential elements that account for its efficacy. The research programme on schizophrenia took twenty years of continuous work before we began to train therapists to deliver the intervention. It is exciting to have reached this advanced stage in the research on depression, the future development of which will be greatly facilitated by this excellent book, which represents the distilled experience of two highly skilled therapists.

SYSTEMIC COUPLE THERAPY AND DEPRESSION

Overture

This book is about the application of systemic ideas and practice to depressed individuals and their partners. It has been written in response to the considerable interest stimulated in the psychotherapeutic and psychiatric communities by the findings of a comparative research study on depression, carried out over a period of many years, in which we participated. In the first two chapters, we describe the findings of the research project and the development of a manual that lays out our approach; we then go on to give individual descriptions of our ways of working with clients, and end with a discussion of our observations in the course of the work, as well as reflections on the general applicability of this approach.

The structure of this book can best be described by means of musical metaphors. The first chapter is symphonic, in that it contains many voices blended together. It sets the theme and describes the historical context and findings of the London Depression Intervention Trial (Leff et al., in press), on which this book is based. Chapter two is a piece of chamber music, perhaps like a violin and piano sonata, fusing our individual voices

1

achieved through our long struggle to create a therapy manual. The aim of writing a detailed therapy protocol was to satisfy the requirements of the research trial whilst at the same time representing our different perspectives—that is, different perspectives as systemic therapists from those of the researchers, and also different perspectives from each other, as different sorts of systemic therapists. Some background voices in this chapter belong to colleagues who are engaged in similar research (Pote et al., 1998; UKCP, 1999) and resonating with their work has been encouraging. Chapters three and four are solo performances, idiosyncratic accounts of our work with depressed persons and their partners. These two chapters are deliberately dissimilar in that their different structure, approach, and style appropriately reflect our differences as therapists. Chapter five is a fugue in which we each take turns to state individual positions, which are then responded to by the other. Sometimes one voice leads and then the other; sometimes the voices are in unison—and at other times they are polyphonic, or even clash a little, as in a modern work of music. We end, we think, in considerable harmony.

CHAPTER ONE

The London Depression
Intervention Trial:
design and findings

The London Depression Intervention Trial (LDIT: Leff et al., in press) was set up in 1991 to compare the effectiveness of antidepressant drugs, individual cognitive behaviour therapy (CBT), and systemic couple therapy. Patients diagnosed as "depressed" by psychiatrists were randomly assigned to one of these three treatment modalities. However, the CBT arm of the trial had to be stopped at an early stage because the drop-out rate was so high (8 out of the first 11 cases). The final comparison, therefore, was between drug therapy and systemic couple therapy and involved 88 subjects who met the research criteria and were taken into treatment.

One of the major findings was that depressed people seen in systemic couple therapy did significantly better than those treated with CBT or antidepressant medication. It was because of these encouraging results for couple therapy that we decided to write this book.

Background of the study

All research projects have their own histories. They come to life in specific contexts, for specific reasons. Julian Leff, professor of psychiatry and an internationally known researcher, has been involved for many years in furthering the understanding and clinical usefulness of the concept of Expressed Emotion (EE) in research on families and persons diagnosed as suffering from schizophrenia (Leff, Kuipers, Berkowitz, Eberleinfries, & Sturgeon, 1982). There has been some research support for the hypothesis that EE might be relevant in working with depressed patients and their key relatives. This led to the setting up of the LDIT to determine whether intervening with a family member or partner might have beneficial effects on the designated patient's depressive symptoms if the partner's EE was reduced.

This is where another piece of history comes in. In the mid-1980s, Julian Leff and the Marlborough Family Service team in London, a group of therapists working systemically in a community setting, jointly engaged in researching the outcome of their therapeutic work. EE was used to measure aspects of the couple (dyadic) relationship, and the study showed that EE (and Critical Comments in particular) was reduced in couples and families presenting problems ranging from emotional and conduct disorders in children, to eating disorders, marital discord, and family violence. These results provided further encouragement to investigate the relationship between depression and EE and to determine whether the existence of such a relationship might inform therapeutic practice. Eia Asen was one of the Marlborough team involved in the study (Asen et al., 1991) and was therefore approached by Julian Leff to set up the pilot phase of the LDIT. Elsa Jones joined the project after the pilot phase.

Because cognitive behaviour therapy and pharmacotherapy with a psychoeducational component had already been manualized, it was necessary for systemic couple therapy also to be described in a manualized form (see chapter two). No controlled studies had been carried out evaluating whether systemic therapy was of any use with depressed patients. Because no standardized treatments existed, the development of a treatment manual for this form of therapy was a precondition for the funding of the study by the body providing the grant—the Medical Research Council.

Version 1 of the manual was exactly one page long, since it seemed impossible to make concrete the art of therapy. However, this version was not acceptable to the researchers, as it was thought to be "too vague". Version 2 went to the opposite extreme: over 100 pages, narrowly printed, obsessionally detailing every possible therapeutic manoeuvre, with form of words, tone, pace of delivery all prescribed. When trying this out, it emerged that not even the writer of the manual could possibly have any hope of adhering consistently to it. At this point, Elsa Jones joined the project and provided a different perspective. Over a period of nine months, new ideas and techniques were introduced and then modified by both of us until agreement had been reached on a version that we could both subscribe to.

Writing a treatment manual is one thing, but adhering to it is another. Adherence to a manual or protocol is important in research so that results can be compared. It makes it possible to replicate research and to assess whether treatment models being compared are significantly different from one another. Consequently, each session was videotaped, and tapes were randomly selected by an independent rater to check for treatment adherence and treatment integrity. This included looking at fifteen sessions with a total time of 1,026 minutes for CBT, thirty-eight sessions with 1,971 minutes for couple therapy, and forty-seven sessions with 1,445 minutes for drug therapy. This research (Schwarzenbach & Leff, 1995) concluded that it was possible to distinguish clearly between different models. Each model was demonstrably characteristic of itself and not of the other models. It was also found that the therapists adhered to the manual but also occasionally used some techniques from other therapies. Therefore, despite our difficulties in coming to terms with writing a manual, this research demonstrated that it was possible to describe what we did in such a way that the description encompassed our work but did not overlap with that of the other modalities.

The LDIT

Method

The LDIT involved an initial baseline assessment of depressed patients and their partners, followed by an intervention (treatment) phase. Patients were assessed at the end of treatment and again after a twelve- to fifteen-month period of no treatment. The treatment phase consisted of a maximum of nine months or twenty sessions for couple therapy and CBT, and one year for antidepressant medication. Patients allocated to one of the treatments were not permitted to receive any other treatment simultaneously. In other words, those patients seen for couple therapy did not receive any antidepressant or other pyschotropic medication. In the twelve months after completion of treatment, it was permitted to offer a maximum of two booster sessions.

Patients had to meet criteria for depression as measured by the Present State examination, the Hamilton Depression Rating Scale, and the Beck Depression Inventory (BDI). The threshold for significant depression on the BDI was set at 11. Partners were assessed on the BDI and the Camberwell Family Interview (Vaughn & Leff, 1976), and patients and partners were assessed on the Dyadic Adjustment Scale. The partner had to be rated as expressing at least two Critical Comments (high EE) during the Camberwell Family Interview (Vaughn & Leff, 1976). In addition to these baseline assessments, all patients—and, in couple therapy, also their partners—were given six-weekly BDI assessments to plot the course of mood changes during the treatment phase. Following termination of treatment, three-monthly BDIs were done by the researchers until the follow-up assessment. Subjects were excluded for a variety of reasons, including psychotic features, bipolar illness, organic brain syndrome, and primary substance abuse. The subjects who were included met the psychiatric criteria for significant depressive illness. Patients allocated to the different treatments were matched on all relevant characteristics, such as age of patient and partner, sex of patient, and chronicity and severity of depression. All therapists of the three different treatment modalities (CBT, antidepressant drugs, systemic couple therapy) agreed that the sample seemed biased towards the heavy end of the spectrum, with many of the patients having long psychiatric histories and being significantly distressed and socially disadvantaged. The presence of particularly difficult patients entering research projects is not an unfamiliar finding, and we discuss some of the implications below.

Results

On a number of different measures, couple therapy proved to be more effective and acceptable than antidepressant medication. Patients participating in couple therapy were less depressed at the end of treatment and on two-year follow-up.

Patients receiving antidepressant medication dropped out at a much more significant rate (56.8%) than those in couple therapy (15%). A fuller discussion of the complexity and wealth of data can be found in the research paper by Leff et al. (in press). A health economic analysis showed that antidepressant treatment is no cheaper than systemic couple therapy.

Figure 1.1 graphically illustrates the differences between the two treatment modalities as measured by the BDI. It can be seen that on average there is a dramatic drop in depressive symptoma-

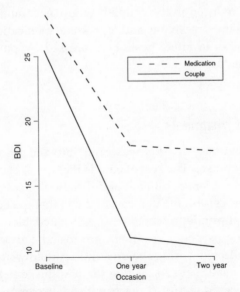

FIGURE 1.1   Mean profiles of couple and medical treatment groups

tology in the couple therapy group, not only at the end of treatment but, perhaps more strikingly, at two-year follow-up.

What do the findings mean?

The major finding of the study has to be the reduction in depression in the patients receiving this diagnosis. However, a number of other findings seem to us worth discussing.

Expressed Emotion

Did EE change during or after the different treatments? The number of Critical Comments, so crucial in the work with families containing a person diagnosed as schizophrenic, was found *not* to be related to change. In some of the couples with dramatic reduction in depressive symptoms, the number of Critical Comments went up, in others nothing changed, and of course there were those where there was a reduction. However, there was a significant change in another dimension of EE: the level of Hostility was significantly reduced in the couples' group as compared with the group of patients receiving antidepressant medication. Systemic therapy appears to affect hostility expressed by partners of depressed patients.

The costs of treatments

A health economic analysis was built into the research project from the very outset. The cost of couple therapy was calculated on the basis of the average number and duration of sessions (12 sessions, 60 minutes) and the unit cost of direct therapist contact time. All prescribed antidepressants (and associated blood tests) plus the prescribing psychiatrist's time were costed. Service utilization data were collected during therapy and on follow-up, covering a range of key health and social care services (in-/out-/day-patient hospital services; day care; contacts with a GP, community psychi-

Table 1. The costs of therapy and service utilization

| | Cost component (£ per month, 1995/96) | | | | | | | |
| | Couple therapy group | | | Drug therapy group | | | Significance (2-tailed t-test) | |
	N	Mean	SD	N	Mean	SD	t value	p value
Treatment period								
A. Therapy	24	106	23	14	48	18	7.51	<0.01
B. Hospital & community	24	25	36	14	78	134	–1.10	0.28
C. Combined cost (A + B)	24	131	38	14	126	139	1.75	0.10
Follow-up period								
D. Hospital & community	27	43	60	21	67	122	–1.34	0.19

atric nurse, social worker, counsellor, etc). Unit costs were attached to these data and aggregated to give a total cost estimate for each study subject. The mean cost of couple therapy was approximately £100 per session and that of drug therapy about half that, £50. However, it emerged that this significantly greater cost of treatment was offset by a reduction in hospital service use costs (£20 less per month in the couple therapy) and community service costs (£33 per month less). In summary, the combined cost of therapy and service turned out to be similar for the two groups (see Table 1.1).

We would like to speculate that the economics of working systemically might be even more striking than emerges from this analysis. First of all, many patients receiving antidepressant medication outside of research projects continue with the drugs for years. Therefore, the long-term costs of prescribing antidepressant medication would in reality be higher. Furthermore, this study did not cost for informal caregiver support by family or others, or for the indirect consequences of depression, such as lost employment. Again, this means that the actual economic benefits of no longer being depressed are greater than can be captured in the health economic analysis undertaken.

The subjects

It is striking that of the 290 individuals with whom the research initially made contact, 196 were excluded for a variety of reasons (no stable relationship, not being depressed, not being willing to accept randomization). Of the 94 taken into the trial a further 6 subsequently rejected the possibility of accepting antidepressants were they to be allocated to the medical arm of the study. Furthermore, for reasons of statistical simplicity, only heterosexual couples were considered.

Again, we venture to speculate that this process of repeated selection and self-selection resulted in a particular group of patients crossing the hurdles into the final stage of being accepted for therapy. What does it mean for a patient—or a referrer on behalf of a patient—to agree to accept any of three very different types of treatment to which they know they will be allocated at random? Most people have some opinion on what might be helpful in addressing their difficulties. To accept the conditions of the study probably means that one has given up hope for oneself or for one's referred patient. This must then have implications for the bias observed by the therapists—namely, that patients tended to belong at the more serious end of the spectrum. Perhaps this is one of the reasons why CBT seemed inappropriate for this group of patients, given that it has established itself as a suitable treatment for depression of recent onset and short duration.

The relatively low drop-out rate in the couple's group has been explained by the researchers as probably due to the greater acceptability of this approach when compared with antidepressant medication. This may well be valid but we think there could also be other reasons. In the first place, when we first met them, many of the partners of the patients diagnosed as depressed expressed their reluctance to participate in therapy (see chapter five), and we had to work hard to facilitate their engagement in the work. This is something that systemic therapists are particularly good at since, from the very beginnings of family therapy, we have set ourselves to learn how to involve family members, who may be reluctant to attend, in a cooperative endeavour focused on the resolution of problems that might at first be seen as being located within an individual. Second, systemic therapy—unlike some other therapeutic approaches—does not have a fixed procedure but works interactively, responsively, and reflexively in relation to the presentation of the client(s). This probably influences the quality of engagement. Third, systemic therapists are always interested in the wider system that forms the context for the symptom and its carrier. This interest may take the form of inviting significant others to sessions, in person or metaphorically, which signals the therapist's conviction that problems and their solutions may be located in the context rather than solely within the client. This context might mean the immediate interpersonal system of the designated patient or the wider context of culture, employment, and so forth. These ideas are explored in more detail in the subsequent chapters, but we mention them here because they may well constitute an explanation for the "acceptability" of systemic couple therapy.

Experiences in this project showed that it is possible to work within a positivist scientific framework without having to compromise the systemic stance. The results when viewed within the dominant scientific discourse prove that systemic couple therapy with depressed patients is effective. We have also found as psychotherapists that it is possible to survive and learn from participation in such a research project.

CHAPTER TWO

The therapy manual

A requirement of the research project was that each treatment modality had to provide a protocol describing its approach. Eia Asen had already started this process during the pilot phase, and both authors then continued to struggle with several more versions. We found the writing of such a protocol difficult partly because of our distaste for pinning down our practice in what seemed a rigid and prescriptive format—psychotherapy is, after all, an art as well as a set of techniques—but also because the two of us orient ourselves at somewhat different ends of the systemic spectrum. Thus Elsa Jones could be described as being placed somewhere in the "post-Milan" group, strongly influenced by feminist and social constructionist ideas (Jones, 1993), whereas Eia Asen occupies a position that draws on a number of different approaches, from structural to strategic to post-Milan therapies (Asen, 1997). Thus the final working document stated that "each therapist is likely to use most of these techniques during the course of therapy with each couple" but some techniques were very unlikely to be used, at least in their pure form, by both therapists. Additionally, experienced therapists are unlikely to be working in a way that reflects a pure model, since, after a significant period as a practitioner, one's style becomes personal and influenced by a continuous learning process from colleagues, clients, and one's own life.

Despite these doubts, it was interesting that the assessment of protocol compliance (Schwarzenbach & Leff, 1995), discussed in chapter one, found that randomly observed videotapes of our work were clearly identifiable as belonging within the parameters of the protocol, and clearly distinct from the individual cognitive behaviour therapy and drugs treatment modalities. One is presumably dealing here with the phenomenon of position influencing perspective, in that small differences will loom large when observed from inside the frame, whereas they will become insignificant to an observer outside the frame.

The original purpose of the manual was to declare the characteristics of the model for the purpose of the researchers. For this book, we have slightly shifted the emphasis in order to make it available to readers who are systemic colleagues, and also to those trainees who will be participating in further stages of research into couples work with depression. The book does not set out to be a textbook of systemic therapy but, rather, to describe a particular application. Some ideas and techniques are described in order to illuminate our work with this particular client group, but in general we take for granted that readers will refer elsewhere for a general systemic background (e.g. Bateson, 1972; Boscolo, Cecchin, Hoffman, & Penn, 1987; Burnham, 1986; Campbell & Draper, 1985; Goldner, 1985; Jones, 1993; Perelberg & Miller, 1990).

A SYSTEMIC APPROACH TO DEPRESSION

A.
Conceptual background

In this model, the depressive symptoms of the designated patient (DP)[1] are conceptualized in interactional terms based on the wide spectrum of systemic family therapy models. The DP is seen as being part of a variety of different contexts, and the various behaviours, including the symptoms, are viewed as being connected with these, which may include patterns in here-and-now relationships and from families of origin, and from other contexts such as the world of work, of society, and of culture. Close relationships are regarded both as influencing and being influenced by the DP and by the symptoms. The responses of family members to the DP may then be seen as helping to maintain, or contributing to, the DP's distress and symptoms. For instance, a DP's partner reacts to the DP's depressive behaviours, and the DP then responds to the partner's reactions. In this way, an elaborate feedback system is generated, affecting the DP's symptoms as well as the behaviours and attitudes of others.

Whilst there is room in this model to accommodate other potentially causative or triggering factors to do with the individual characteristics and experiences of the DP (past and present, physical, psychological, or cultural), it is, however, assumed that the present depressive behaviours are primarily maintained by the various contexts of which the DP is part—above all, the family and the profes-

---

[1] The term DP is used here to indicate that the persons so designated (by themselves, by family members, or by professionals) are being seen by therapists within a medical referral system. From a systemic point of view, a diagnosis is not a discovery of a reality, but an agreed-upon label or professional shorthand used for convenience of communication. Naming is not a neutral activity: those who take or are given the right to name others are likely to be in a position of power and privilege in relation to those named.

15

sional helping system—and that a focus on these may offer the shortest route to a dissolving of the DP's difficulties.

Interactionally framed, depression could be construed to develop in the following way: an event occurs (illness, redundancy, birth of child, etc.) that makes a demand on the individual(s) to adapt. Intrapsychic and/or inter-personal factors (learned styles of adaptation, family patterns and "rules", the relative presence or absence of maladaptive "fit" developed interactively over time), as well as the range of contextual factors named above, enable some individuals to deal with such demands better than others. Those who are less able to adapt may begin to exhibit depressive symptoms or behaviours. These in turn represent stressors to which the spouse and family will respond. Depending on certain couple and family structures and dynamics, there may be quite varied responses: some families may tolerate depression, whereas others may be extremely critical of and impatient with their member's depressive behaviours. A special focus on what is perceived as the depressed person's negative behaviours can increase "depression" and associated phenomena, some of which may subsequently be labelled as "attention-seeking" by a partner. The ensuing couple interaction can further affect the DP's depression. For example, attempts to help DPs to resolve their depression by drawing their attention to non-depressive aspects of their lives—"looking on the bright side"—may increase their sense of isolation and not being understood, thus augmenting their depression; the attempted solution thereby becomes part of the further exasperation of the problem. On the other hand, helping, caring, and caretaking responses on the part of family members may lead to the "caretaker/patient" roles within the family being maintained even when the depressive behaviours no longer have their original significance.

The main aim of a systemic approach to couple therapy for depression is, then, to contextualize the presenting symptom(s)—that is, to place them in the context of the individual's current and past relationships with family members and/or significant others, as well as of social and cultural factors and discourses. Systemic couple therapy aims to help the DP and her or his partner to get new perspectives on the presenting problem(s), to attach different meanings to the depressive behaviours, or to experiment with new ways of relating to one another. It is postulated that if the couple change their interaction, the symptom may change. This change can be brought about by changes at the level of meaning *or* behaviour, since it is assumed that these are reflexively looped with one another, and change in one will affect change in the other—without "insight" having to be a necessary precursor to change.

When people approach (or are referred to) professionals for help, it can usually be assumed that their own problem-solving skills have not proved useful. It is therefore the therapist's task to explore with the DP and the partner/family how they have come to be "stuck" in a pattern of interaction that seems inextricably linked to symptomatic behaviour. The therapist attempts to elicit together with the couple (family) what resources they have for achieving new and different interaction patterns that will not include the symptom and associated behaviours.

The therapist does not impose normative (or other) views about couple functioning in general, nor about the specific solutions that might be applicable to this couple in particular. Instead, the therapist maintains a stance of open-minded curiosity ("neutrality" towards ideas, persons, and outcomes), which leads to an exploration with the couple of the history and meanings of their current situation and of their previous attempted solutions and impasses.

The process of circular interviewing (see Section C3 below) used in systemic therapy is assumed to disrupt current patterning—that is, to have a perturbing effect that will serve to loosen up interaction and communication patterns that the couple themselves have identified or experienced as rigid or undesirable. While the therapist's questions are in part intended to suggest possible new ways of viewing or doing things, as well as to explore the consequences of maintaining "familiar" patterns, the choices of when, what, and how to change rest with the couple. It is assumed that individuals, alone and in interaction with significant others, have resources that will enable them to make changes that will be more adaptive while still coherent with their belief and value systems, family traditions, and so on, and that they themselves are better placed to do this than the therapist(s). Thus, in summary, it is the therapist's task to enable couples to see that there are different routes that can be taken, rather than to tell them which specific route to follow. The therapist acts as a catalyst rather than a social engineer; the aim therefore is *not* to "educate" the couple or teach them how to do things "best", but to empower them to apply their own solutions.

B.
The process of systemic couple therapy

Before meeting the therapist for the first time, the DP and his or her partner would already have had meetings with the researchers in which the couple will have been assessed on various measures (see chapter one), received explanations of the therapy and research activities, agreed to accept allocation to any of the three models being compared, and given their consent to videotaping of the therapy sessions. Additionally, agreement for purposes of publications will have been obtained. The following is a general schema of the way in which the therapy would generally be expected to go—that is, the general "shape" of systemic therapy with a couple where one member carries a psychiatric diagnosis.

1.   Early sessions

While the necessity for engagement (see Section B2 below) is always in the therapist's awareness, it is of central importance in the earliest sessions. Without a sense of trust, clarity, and safe boundaries, clients cannot begin to talk confidingly with the stranger who is the therapist. Thus, the therapist signals from the very beginning—by overt communication and via body language and other non-verbal communications and by even-handedness, willingness to hear both points of view, and a neutrality towards outcomes and multiple perspectives—that she or he is someone with whom a containing space can be created in which the DP's and the couple's dilemmas can be explored. It is helpful to the therapist if the setting echoes this; however, since some of the work in the research project was of necessity done in the rather un-therapeutic setting of an academic research institute linked to a psychiatric hospital, it has to be admitted that good joining (see Section C2 below) can often transcend an unsupportive environment.

At the outset, the therapist explores the problem definitions of the couple and their reports of those of significant others, thus simultaneously obtaining a picture of the network of significant relationships within which the problem is contextualized. This may be done with the help of a genogram (see Section C8 below). Exploring the problem definition has behavioural and meaning-associated elements; the therapist will seek information about how the problem has manifested itself over time, its effects on all concerned, and how others respond to it, as well as what meanings are attributed to it by the various participants in the couple's social network. Thus, current patterns are linked to multigenerational patterns in the past, and the couple and therapist strive for a new understanding of what actions and ideas contribute to paralysing them in the present. This may have the effect of couples wishing to experiment with new behaviours in their search for new solutions to familiar predicaments. Sessions in this phase are likely to be spaced closely together (e.g. at weekly or fortnightly intervals).

While tracking the sequences of problematic behaviours and interactions, attention will also be paid to any reported successes in the present and in the past. Understanding how the couple may at times have coped positively with setbacks introduces hope into the discussion and helps the therapist to gain insight into the couple's style and resources (see Section C5 below). It is also useful to know what solutions have been tried before—including a history of contacts with other helping professionals—in order to know what has been useless, as well as what might have seeds of usefulness for future implementation. This kind of discussion also begins to imply a different future, which might at this stage, for the DP and his or her partner, exist in a hypothetical dimension only (see Section C3 below).

Systemic therapy is characterized by a collaborative or co-constructive stance; the therapist's style is tentative and at all stages invites the client to cooperate, question, and give feedback on the therapist's work as well as on tasks and events from between-session intervals. The therapist needs to be sensitive to issues affecting the therapeutic relationship, whether these arise from clients' dynamics or from matters related primarily to "self-of-therapist" dilemmas (see chapter five). Thus, the clients are active participants who together with the therapist attempt to construct new meanings, to achieve an observer perspective on their relationship patterns, and to develop new behaviours. In the early sessions, part of the therapist's work will be aimed at inviting the clients to participate in such a style of interaction. This will include an exploration of the clients' goals for change. While these goals, and therefore the corresponding definition of the task of therapy, may change as time goes on, it is important that this should continue to be an overt focus for discussion. Otherwise, particularly in a setting of psychiatric diagnosis and referral by professionals, the client may well remain in a passive role as the recipient of the intentions of others.

2.   Middle sessions

At this stage in therapy, the exploration is likely to be less tightly problem-focused and to concentrate more on the wider patterns that are maintaining and are being maintained by the problem. This altered emphasis may represent an attempt to widen the focus of therapy in order to shift a still intractable problem, or to stimulate change in the couple's relationship with each other (and others) in order to prevent recurrence of the problem, or to begin to focus on "quality-of-life" questions.

By this stage the clients are likely to be more active in setting the agenda for therapy, reporting on their observations of problematic as well as desired interactions in their day-to-day lives, and making decisions about the optimum spacing of sessions (which is likely to be at longer intervals now) and the design of interval tasks and so on. While the time-frame of therapy will always be moving backwards and forwards from dilemmas in the present to connections in the past of the couple and the "luggage" they may be carrying from their families of origin to the feared or desired future, it is likely that this stage of therapy will be predominantly focused on the present and on the detailed work of altering habitual patterns of behaviour and of belief that may, by now, have been identified as reinforcing and maintaining unwanted feeling states or actions, including the DP's depression.

This may be a time when it seems apposite to have some individual meetings with the DP and her or his partner (see Section C11b below) or to invite other family members to attend sessions.

The consolidation, by now, of a working alliance between therapist and clients means that in this phase the therapist can feel more confident about using techniques likely to trigger major perturbation and change for clients, such as feed-forward questions, challenging, enactment, reframing, amplified use of stories and metaphors, tasks and non-verbal techniques, and so on, as discussed in Section C. There is likely to be an ever-strengthening focus on client strengths and resources and on the amplification of whatever small changes may be present and of a constant shifting of responsibility and "ownership" of change from therapist to clients. It is also the phase in which therapist and clients may have the most frustrating experiences of being stuck, of wrestling with intractable difficulties, and of despair. If progress is being made, it is important to measure this against the original goals of therapy: are these being achieved, and do they need to be renegotiated?

3.   Ending sessions

If therapy is producing positive results as far as the clients are concerned this phase is likely to be characterized by review of the work done and by anticipation and prevention of relapse—that is, identifying patterns that in the past have led up to a depressive episode, finding markers to allow the couple to be alert to repetition, and rehearsing new strategies for dealing with it differently. This may include an unpacking, more explicitly than before, by the therapist of his or her own understandings and hypotheses about client dilemmas, which can act as a sort of "take-home" package for the clients. Sessions in the later phases of therapy are likely to be more widely spaced than before (several weeks, if not months) and may include booster sessions after completion of the therapy (see chapter one).

As part of the preparation for ending therapy, it may be useful to discuss the role of the therapist in the couple's life. This might include a consideration of how the couple will, in the future, continue the work started in the therapy, and it will, therefore, lead on to hypothetical explorations of future scenarios, hopes, fears, strategies for actions, and the development and maintenance of new narratives and beliefs.

In Section C, a variety of technical aspects are listed and described in some detail. Each therapist is likely to use most of these techniques during the course of therapy with each couple, though individual differences between the therapists are likely to result in certain techniques being used more frequently than others.

C.
Technical aspects of systemic couple therapy

1.   Hypothesizing

Before seeing a couple for the first time, and before, during, and after subsequent sessions, therapists formulate and test working hypotheses (Selvini Palazzoli, Boscolo, Cecchin, & Prata, 1980a). These hypotheses are preliminary attempts to explain the DP's presenting symptoms in terms of the contexts within which they occur, and the hypotheses include, as more information emerges during the course of therapy, all the significant participants and known events and relationships in an interactive pattern that offers both an explanation and possible solutions.

There are several reasons for making hypothesizing an overt and formal part of the therapist's functioning. First, it openly acknowledges the therapist's assumptions, prejudices, values, and hunches. Second, hypothesizing allows therapists to keep track of their organizing ideas, which can then be viewed and modified in the light of the feedback from the couple. In this way, the continuous formulation (and refutation) of hypotheses keeps the therapists alert to the active part they are playing in the shaping of the therapeutic reality, for the therapists' interviewing and other actions are part of what elicits the particular account the couple will give (Jones, 1993). As systemic therapy becomes increasingly co-constructive and transparent in style, it becomes more likely that a therapist will, with careful regard for timing and language, share hypotheses with clients, so that all the participants in the therapeutic encounter are able to join together in considering potential meanings within the system.

Hypotheses are working guidelines for organizing the therapist's work; thus, two or three hypotheses are entertained simultaneously to guard against the temptation to regard a hypothesis as a factual statement. In this way, the therapist's interest and curiosity will be kept alive, thereby warding off excessive certainty as well as reducing the risk of engaging in stereotyped and routine work. Hypothesizing has developed in the context of teamwork; this is particularly so in the practice of Milan-oriented therapists, who are likely to follow the classic "five-part" structure or its more recent innovations. (Andersen, 1987; Selvini Palazzoli, Boscolo, Cecchin, & Prata, 1978). Therapists working without the benefit of teams have found that structures developed with teams can continue to be useful for lone practitioners; of these structures, those making formal space for the review of hypotheses may be the most important.

The central function of hypothesizing can be said to be, firstly, organizing the therapist's thinking and, secondly, making this organization overt. The focus of hypothesizing is the search for an understanding of how the clients' dilemmas may connect to the relevant system. Working hypotheses guide the therapist's conversation in the quest for an adequate description of the clients' situation; fuller systemic hypotheses allow therapists and clients to focus on what needs to change.

The many tentative and partial hypothetical ideas that follow will not in themselves constitute a coherent hypothesis. In order to construct useful working hypotheses, such partial speculations need to be knitted together into a coherent possible narrative describing the clients' dilemmas and the roles played in these by all participants; these hypotheses can then be tested, changed, and developed in response to feedback from the therapy sessions (Selvini Palazzoli et al., 1980a).

Listed below are some of the generic hypotheses and questions that we tended to have in mind about clients seen in the depression study. These, of course, have to be amplified in the light of the unique circumstances of the specific couple. Many of these hypotheses are overlapping, and the list is not an exhaustive one. Although, because of the study design discussed in chapter one, the

focus here, as throughout the book, is on heterosexual couple relationships, many of these hypotheses would also apply to DPs not in
couple relationships or to those in same-sex relationships;

1a: *The meaning of depression*

Depression is assumed to have meaning that can be viewed as
significant at the level of

- communication (e.g. as a message to the partner that he
  or she should be more involved);
- metaphor for family events (e.g. keeping alive the
  memory of a deceased family member);
- system maintenance (e.g. to prevent partner or children
  from leaving home);
- position in the system (e.g. the relationship with the
  partner around depression will maintain and confirm
  previous relationship patterns).

1b: *Depression in the context of the research project*

- Why are these clients willing to be blindly allocated to
  any one of three treatment modalities?
  —no choice, given their relationship with helping pro-
    fessions and their social context
  —strong faith in professional expertise
  —fatalism regarding relative hopefulness of any treat-
    ment
- Why are these clients willing to attend as a couple?
  —belief that there is a relationship issue
  —desire to "support" partner
  —threat to leave the relationship by the DP if partner
    does not attend
  —wish to form coalition with professional to label
    depressed partner
  —wish to form coalition with professional to change
    non-depressed partner
  —and/or for reasons listed in 1a above

1c: *Depression in the context of the referral*

- What about this patient led to this referrer making a referral to this research project?

  —trust in scientific and/or therapeutic value of project

  —off-loading of difficult patient for whom there is little hope

  —fatalism regarding the relative hopefulness of any treatment

- Why has the referral been made now?

  —increasing demands made by patient on referrer

  —referrer's frustrated normative expectations (e.g. regarding time taken to recover)

1d: *Depression in social/cultural context*

- What are the social factors that may precipitate and maintain depression?

  —finance, housing, unemployment, social isolation, and marginalization

  —racism and discrimination on the grounds of group identity, membership of marginalized and victimized subcultures, and social networks

- What are the gender issues for patients in couple relationships that precipitate or maintain depression?

  In women:

  —marriage, single parenthood, maternal age, and age of child(ren)

  —problems of identity, changed couple relationships, and diminished choices when children leave home

  —dilemmas associated with sexuality and fertility

  —the effects of assumptions about women's roles on work identity and status

  —identity dilemmas associated with job pressure and job loss

  —violence within context of power differentials

—financial vulnerability

In men:

—identity dilemmas associated with job pressure and job loss

—problems of identity, changed couple relationships, and diminished choices when children leave home

—dilemmas associated with sexuality and fertility

—depression masked by alcohol misuse and violence

—changing gender roles (e.g. fear of acknowledging dependence on women, loss of traditional support)

—financial insecurity

In both:

—history of abuse, betrayal , despair in relationships, triggered by life stages or events

1e: *Depression in family context*

• What precipitates depression?

—predictable life-cycle issues (e.g. birth of child, retirement)

—unexpected life-cycle issues (e.g. sudden death, chronic illness)

—impact of external events (e.g. redundancy)

• What maintains depression?

—"break from ordinary life"

—"glue" for the relationship

—"punishment for past sins"

—regulating distance between partners

—protecting partner

—controlling partner

—keeping family of origin involved

—giving a job to "retired" parent(s)

—once-meaningful interactional patterns have become habitual and unhelpful

—fear of change

—attempted solutions have become part of the problem

2.   Joining and engagement

Joining is the process of accommodation between therapist and
couple, the search for "fit" that will be good enough to allow the
difference that will be introduced by the therapist to be explored
in a context of safety. It can be described as the formation of a
therapeutic alliance, the development of rapport—the non-specific
essential ingredient of all therapy. While a therapist may be more
conscious of using joining techniques initially, joining is an ongoing
process that needs to be maintained throughout therapy and aims
both at establishing engagement and facilitating change. Joining is
established through the use of technique integrated with the therapist's presentation of self (Minuchin & Fishman, 1981). Some
specific aspects are highlighted below.

2a: The therapist may engage in some "social" conversation at
      times and particularly in the first session, to put couples at
      their ease (e.g. "Did you find it easy to get here?"). Part of
      this process may also be accomplished by discussion of
      the context of therapy (e.g. length of sessions, use of
      videotape, therapists's and couple's expectations, etc.).
      On the other hand, early engagement may take place in
      the course of the initial exploration of what brings the
      clients to therapy.

2b: The therapist's communication and engagement skills are
      essential elements in facilitating change. For the purposes
      of joining, attention is paid to the way in which even-
      handed attention is given to both partners and to their
      views and belief systems. Thus, even if these views are
      opposed to each other, by giving equal weight to each the
      therapist will, at one and the same time, communicate an
      interest in understanding each partner and will begin to
      offer the therapeutic suggestion that more than one point

of view may be valid. This stance of even-handedness, and the sense of "being in tune", will be communicated via words (e.g. reflecting language used by the couple themselves), conscious posture (e.g. mirroring), tone, and so forth.

2c: It is important to check whether the therapist has understood what people are saying (e.g. "Let me just check with you that I've got this right . . ."). Thus, repetition, in slightly changed language, offers confirmation of being understood, emphasizes what has been said, and offers the opportunity to begin to frame the couple's presentation somewhat differently (e.g. from "He always deliberately tries to hurt me . . ." to "When it feels to you as if he is trying deliberately to hurt you . . .").

2d: The therapist attempts to maintain a stance of neutrality towards ideas and thus does not directly challenge statements made by members of the couple even if they appear to be critical or negative.

2e: Sympathetic, non-judgemental listening is a technique of engagement as well as a feature, throughout therapy, of the therapist's stance. That is, a systemic frame means that the therapist does not seek to attribute blame but, instead, to understand respectfully how couples, despite what appear to be their best efforts, have become stuck in difficult relationship patterns.

2f: "Joining" in this particular research project also means an initial acceptance on the therapist's part of the problem definition with which the couple arrive at the first (and subsequent) session. As they have been told by the referrer, as well as the research team, that the DP will receive treatment for his or her "depression" or "depressive illness", the partner of the DP will often assume that he or she has only come along as an "informant", "co-therapist", or "for support". Premature challenging of this stance or early reframing of the partner as "part of the problem" needs to be avoided to prevent drop-out. (See chapter five for a fuller discussion.)

2g: Throughout the therapy, the therapist monitors the way in which her or his own presence and presentation may be perceived by the clients, especially if this is likely to prove an obstacle to the establishment of a trusting working relationship. For example, the therapist's perceived ethnicity, race, class, age, gender, and so on may act for the client as an obstacle to joining (see chapter five).

3.   Circular interviewing

The *theory* on which the technique of circular interviewing is based is one of circular causality: there is an assumption that human behaviour can best be understood from a point of view that regards actions as both responses to other actions *and* the triggers for further actions. While it is possible to describe behaviour so as to show a lineal connection between cause and effect (e.g. "she is depressed because her partner has lost interest in her"), a circular construction is less likely to lead to ideas of blame and more likely to enable couples to alter their interactions and belief systems (e.g. regardless of who "first" got depressed or lost interest—even if it were possible to establish that—they can both be said to be involved in a circular loop where one person's depression triggers the other's withdrawal of interest, and/or vice versa).

The *practice* of interviewing follows a circular (or spiralling) pattern, where the feedback to the therapist's question will influence and shape the therapist's next question, and so on. This is a purposive and responsive interviewing style: purposive because the therapist is central as the primary conductor of the session and asker of questions, yet responsive to feedback and openings offered by the couple; thus, both therapist and couple together construct a new understanding of the situation.

Circular interviewing involves a particular interest in questions of difference, since it is through the perception of difference that we construct new information, and different perceptions of self and others become possible. There are various questioning techniques that make it possible for therapist and couple to explore issues of difference and the definition of relationships, such as comparison questions, ranking questions, triadic questions, and so forth. The answers to such questions will stimulate further discussion via the exploration of the responses of participants to differences or similarities in their perceptions of relationships and events (Jones, 1993; Penn, 1985; Selvini Palazzoli et al., 1980a; Tomm, 1987, 1988).

By participating in such an interview, the couple perceive themselves through the eyes of the other; not only may they hear the other's view differently, but their own views, expressed in this context, may look different to them as they engage in an observer perspective on their own situation. Thus, for the therapist and the couple, their interest and curiosity about one another remain stimulated, and changed perceptions of actions or relationships may lead to new and different behaviours and relationships, as well as a re-examination of belief systems that had to date been held with firm conviction.

A special sub-category of this style of questioning is known as *hypothetical questions*. These are particularly useful when individuals or couples are locked in a rigid stance of blaming about who is "at fault" or "ill" and who is not, or where the effect of a symptom such as depression has been to "freeze time", so that it is difficult for clients to have a sense of a viable future (Boscolo & Bertrando, 1993). In the face of such a stuck interactional pattern, the therapist can proceed via an "as-if" stance, which makes it possible to consider change in fantasy, even if it does not—yet—seem possible in reality. *Feed-forward questions* (Penn, 1985) are a particular form of hypothetical questions, where couples are invited to project current relationship patterns and problems into the future and consider the effects of such lack of change on their future lives. This may help to resolve such patterns or to illuminate the feared consequences of change, which form part of the stuckness of the couple system. The effect of circular questioning is:

- To invite the couple's curiosity about the history, context, and pattern of their unsatisfactory interactions, which includes the depressive symptoms. Just as the therapist gains an understanding of how these interactions fit together to result in a relationship pattern that is stressful to the couple, so the couple themselves see their situation differently, make new connections, and see new opportunities for change and flexibility.

- To disrupt and perturb set patterns of thinking and action, functioning as an intensive but contained challenge to the couple's previously held views. Thus, while overtly it may seem less challenging than some more directive techniques (see Section C7), it tends to have similar effects—namely, of altering the balance in the relationship by interrupting habitual patterns.

4. Enactment

In order to understand a couple's usual transactional patterns, the therapist can ask the couple to enact a transaction within the session (Minuchin, 1974). This can take the form of a discussion between the couple, staging a familiar argument, making a decision, comforting one another or whatever. The purposes of enactments are:

- To enable the therapist to see how the couple interact rather than hearing them describe how they believe it happens.
- To propel transactions beyond their usual thresholds in order to test the flexibility of the system.
- To enable the participants to try out different repertoires of transacting in a safe environment.

Initially, the therapist observes, looking for spontaneously repeating sequences. He or she then focuses on a specific issue:

4a: Raising the possibility of the couple to interact around this.

("I notice that this is something that causes you both stress . . . would it be useful if you talk about this here now? . . . So, if you think it might be useful why don't you both do that . . . ignore me just for a minute, pretend I'm not here . . . just have the sort of argument about money that you have at home . . . I will sit back and see what happens.")

4b: Prolonging the time sequence.

("What would happen if you kept this going until you have reached an agreement? . . . Do it if you want to . . .")

4c: Blocking parts of the transaction.

("Don't involve me . . . this is between the two of you", "I notice that you now talk about someone who is not here . . . perhaps that is helpful, perhaps it is not? Do you both now want to discuss whether it is more useful for you to talk to each other about what's upsetting . . . or to play safe and talk about X? Both fine, from my point of view . . .")

4d: Exploring alternative transactions.

("I notice that somehow you, Mrs X, never finish your sentences . . . is that the way you want it? . . . No? . . . How would you like it to be. . . . What would happen if you did it differently then. . . . Do it, if you both want to . . . ignore me. . . . What is it that gets your husband to interrupt you . . . is that the way you want it? No? . . . Well, why don't you find a way of blocking him . . . if that's what you want . . .")

These techniques are employed to help the couple to find new resolutions in the "here-and-now" of the session (Minuchin & Fishman, 1981).

4e: A form of enactment that may be useful in couple therapy consists of a therapist interrupting a customary escalating interaction between partners by engaging one of the partners in a dialogue with herself—for example, a man begins a jealous and potentially intimidating interrogation about his partner's telephone conversation (for a clinical example, see chapter three), or a woman berates her partner for a failure in relation to child-care. By, so to speak, taking the partner's usual place, the therapist is able to challenge the habitual patterns of the interaction, because of the different role she or he occupies in the system, and so to help lead the interaction to a different and perhaps more positive outcome. This means that the partner engaged in the discussion has the opportunity of travelling the same route with a different end-point (e.g. not violence or withdrawal) and the "non-engaged" partner has the opportunity for reflective observation and role modelling.

5. *Focusing on strengths*

Systemic therapy rests on an assumption that all systems, and all participants in systems, do what they can and must do, given the limitations and possibilities of their history, context, and understanding of the situation. Moreover, it is assumed that all people have resources and strengths, unique to themselves, which are likely to lead to more creative and appropriate solutions than any arrived at by the therapist alone. Each couple has elements in their own culture which, if understood and utilized, can become levers to actualize and expand their behavioural and experiential repertoire (Minuchin, 1974; Papp, 1984). Some ways of allowing access to these strengths are the following:

5a: Identifying competence in both individuals as well as in the couple relationship, and pinpointing behaviours that have positive effects on daily relational satisfaction.

("What is it that you can do to please your partner?")

5b: Identifying past positive elements in their interaction (e.g. exploring how they have successfully supported each other during crises in the past; exploring what attracted them to each other originally).

5c: Reframing. This is a technique that aims to give an alternative meaning to events that fits the events as well as the explanation previously subscribed to by the couple but contains some leverage for change (for a more detailed discussion, see Section C9).

5d: Searching for fluctuations of or exceptions (de Shazer, 1985) to the depressive behaviour and framing these positively as potential solutions.

("I'm interested in the times when it happens less, or when it does not happen at all. So when you are doing that . . . it doesn't happen.")

Couples can also be asked to monitor exceptions to negative patterns between sessions (see Section C10 below).

5e: Focusing on positives. The therapist will at times try to discourage conversation that is relentlessly problem-focused or involves the couple complaining about each other and will try to enhance talk that looks at positives, solutions, or small changes (de Shazer, 1985). For example, when someone is exclusively focused on the gloomiest part of his or her life, the therapist could use subjective scales to turn the couple's attention towards some positive aspects.

("If, on a scale from 1 to 10, 10 being the way you feel when things are really bad, you had to say how you felt when things were a bit better ... where would you place yourself/your partner? When was the last time that happened? What did you do to make that happen? When and how could you do more of that?")

5f: In addition to the specific interventive techniques described above, the therapist's use of the nuances of language and interaction can also act to enhance clients' sense of their own strengths and competence. By offering the clients choices, enhancing the opportunities for exercizing sound judgement, asking for feedback, showing genuine interest in the clients' views, even when (or especially when!) they differ from those of the therapist, and generally indicating a belief in the clients' resources, no matter how hidden or unused, the therapist enhances the likelihood that therapy will become a respectful and positively collaborative experience (Jones, 1996; Papp, 1984).

6.   *Problem solving*

At specific stages of therapy, a problem-solving approach (Haley, 1976) may be indicated (see also Section C10 below). To get a precise definition of the problem, the therapist needs to *track* how problematic events happen. The couple is encouraged to describe a sequence of events that leads to conflict or depression. The therapist then searches for the steps or events that precede what has been described to find the "first" step in the sequence. The couple is asked to identify at what point evasive action could have been taken and requested to consider how they could re-act in similar future situations. The following model can be used:

- Agreeing on the exact nature of the problem sequence.
- Specifying desired outcomes (goals).
- Listing past (failed) solutions.
- Tracking pre-problem sequence of events.
- Identifying early preventive action/re-solution.
- Brainstorming about other possible solutions, highlighting advantages and disadvantages of each proposed solution.
- Choosing one specific solution.
- Formulating a detailed plan to implement this solution.
- Speculating about the consequences of implementing a specific plan, and discussing how to review outcome.

7.   Challenging

Individuals, couples, and families all develop over time their own way of seeing things, or of constructing their own "scripts". Such fixed belief systems and/or behaviours can be challenged by the therapist so as to facilitate the emergence of new viewpoints or interactions. Generally, the therapist will comment on observed sequences of interaction and, following feedback from the couple, proceed to use a variety of different challenging techniques.

> **7a:**   *Unbalancing* (Minuchin, 1974) is a technique used to deliberately disequilibrate the family organization, by temporarily joining and supporting one individual at the (apparent) "expense" of the spouse, by enhancing the former's view, commiserating with her or his predicament, and so forth.
>
> ("I notice that every time you talk, your husband stops you or says things that I think may put you down. Perhaps

I'm wrong. Is that the way you see it? Is that the way you want it? So, if you don't—how is it that you allow your husband to put you down all the time? What would happen if you stopped him next time that happened?")

7b: *Intensification* (Minuchin, 1974) is the technique of "putting the heat on"—increasing the affective component of a transaction by increasing the time in which the couple is involved in such a transaction (see *enactment*, Section C4), or frequent repetition of the same message, or by physically or emotionally altering the distance between the couple.

("I can see that you want to give up now . . . what would happen if you didn't, if you kept going, even if things become un-comfortable?" "Do you think it might be useful to keep going—so if you think that, why don't you keep it going?")

7c: *Testing boundaries* (Minuchin & Fishman, 1981) is a way of challenging each individual's and the couple's perceived lack or abundance of private space, their way of allowing differentness to emerge, their ability to be close, their mutual emotional responsiveness, their way of making decisions and use of hierarchies.

("How is it that you allow his mother to dictate how you conduct your marriage? Is he married to his mother or to you?")

7d: *Disrupting.* If a DP specializes in monologues or prolonged episodes of depressive venting, then the therapist may challenge this, initially by inviting the partner to join in.

("How do you respond to this?" "What is your view on this?")

7e: *Perturbation* (Jones, 1993; Maturana & Varela, 1988; Tomm, 1987). Circular interviewing acts as a generator of information about couple functioning, but it also acts to disrupt system organization because of the way in which it allows new connections and juxtapositions to be made

by clients, introduces the element of time, including imagined futures, and invites the participants into an observer stance in relation to their own patterns. This
disruption challenges ("perturbs") the organization of the
system and makes it likely that new patterns, not structured around existing symptoms and problems, may be
found. In this way of working, the therapist will be active
in the use of challenging and persistent circular exploration of themes, but less active (than in 7a–7d above) in
finding solutions.

8.   *Family life-space techniques*

The construction of a *genogram* or family tree (Burnham, 1986;
McGoldrick & Gerson, 1985) is a powerful way of contextualizing
the symptom, the DP, and the couple. Here, it is not the final result
(namely, an elaborately completed tree) that is important, but the
process of constructing it and the questions that guide the couple to
make new discoveries and connections. A genogram may be drawn
up in the session or given to the couple as an inter-session task,
or the therapist may ask questions guided by a "genogram in
the head". How formally or informally genogram work is done will
depend on the therapist's view of the couple, but three-generational
patterning is always of interest in couple therapy.

Particular attention is paid to signs or symptoms of depression on
both sides of the couple's family tree, exploring how different people and generations coped with those symptoms, the effect that
depressive symptoms and behaviours had on others, and the coping
mechanisms used. Connections with the DP's symptomatology and
the couple's predicament can then be made. With the genogram "in
sight", relationship patterns—such as distance and closeness, coalitions, boundaries, and so on—and the meanings that such patterns
may have in the here-and-now for the couple can be explored.

The *family circles method* (Geddes & Medway, 1977) is an exercise that both partners are asked to do simultaneously. Each is
requested to draw a large circle and is told: "That's your life—now
put the people and things that are important in your life inside it.
Draw a circle for each of these, and don't forget to put yourself in as

well." People will visually represent how they see themselves in relation to others, to work, to hobbies, and so forth. Once completed, this task lends itself to a variety of interventions: the couple can compare their respective pictures and question one another, comparing areas of agreement and disagreement. Questions regarding change can be raised in a concrete way by considering which aspects of the circle(s) need to be changed, what would replace it, how one would have to go about bringing about change, and so on.

There are other visual techniques that encourage patients to make diagrammatic representations of their past, present, and/or future life. These techniques usually engage clients with one another as they cannot help commenting on the partner's pictures, thus challenging each others' perceptions and discussing how to do things differently in the future.

9.   Reframing

Reframing is the technique by which the therapist changes the conceptual and emotional setting in which a situation is experienced and places it in another frame that fits the "facts" of the same situation equally well, thereby changing its meaning and thus potentially the behaviours of the participants (Watzlawick, Weakland, & Fisch, 1974). One of the therapists' intentions when reframing is to change from a frame that is implicitly unalterable to a frame that is implicitly flexible and open to change. Changing the frame of reference against which a given event is perceived also changes how it is judged. Judgements such as healthy–sick, sane–mad, physical–psychological, personal–interpersonal, good–bad, and so forth have a tendency to pin down individuals and couples to fixed roles, which can result in stuck and rigid patterns of interaction. Relabelling someone's depression as "anger", or, in other circumstances, as an "act of kindness to the partner", can have dramatic effects on spouse interaction.

Reframing may in practice have been preceded by observations about the couple's interactions and communication patterns, with reference to quantity, quality and direction of communication, affective tone, boundaries, or coalitions and alliances. Such an initial "frame" deliberately singles out and names a specific interactional sequence which may then, at a later stage, be referred to when reframing it—for example, "I notice that whenever you get upset about something in your life your wife starts crying", or "I notice that you don't look at one another when you talk to each other".

Reframing outlines identifiable "functions" of the symptom—that is, protection of aspects of the family organization from changes due to family life-cycle development and other crises of loss or addition. Reframing is more often positive: for example, "If you were less depressed, your partner might not be prepared for it: he may just like being the one who can do everything . . . maybe he'd get depressed if you were to become too competent." However, reframing may also aim to place something in a more negative light: for example, "Depressed persons can seem powerful to others—there is some considerable comfort to be found in the familiar certainty of the depressed person's discomfort."

Positive reframing overlaps with the idea of "positive (or logical) connotation" (Jones, 1993; Selvini Palazzoli et al., 1978) in which an attempt is made to find a description of the actions of the participants in a system, and particularly of the symptom-carrier, which describes these behaviours as necessary to the maintenance and survival of the system. This would involve exploring ideas about the feared "risk" to the couple and family of change and the loss of the symptom—for example, fear of the break-up of relationships, pain at the loss of special closeness, dread of taking responsibility for current situations or past disasters, and so on. This is based on the assumption that people make the best choices they can, given the constraints of their situation; this means that a known distress may seem preferable to a feared consequence of change.

10. Inter-session tasks ("homework")

Inter-session tasks have the purpose of continuing some of the work initiated in the session afterwards in the couple's own home setting (Minuchin, 1974; Selvini Palazzoli, Boscolo, Cecchin, & Prata, 1977, 1980b); one of the consequences is to anchor change within the everyday lives of clients, thus also giving them a greater sense of mastery and "ownership". Tasks create a framework within which the couple is requested to function, pinpointing or dramatizing certain interactions. With couples where one partner is depressed, the following are examples of tasks that may be prescribed:

- A controlled argument about a specified agenda once-weekly at a set time for a set period.

- Diary keeping (separately or jointly) of certain observable activity, such as "worst moods and people's responses", or "guessing when patient is feeling well and noticing and observing the circumstances".

- Have "unusual" outing.

- Prescription of "once-weekly physical closeness" or "odd-days and even-days" strategy (the latter involves encouraging the couple to experiment with new behaviours on "odd days" of the week and to revert to old practices on "even" days).

- Prescription of more autonomy for patient around specific issues (shopping, pacifying in-laws etc.).

- Pretend techniques: these techniques attempt to encourage the partners to experiment with seeing and perceiving one another differently. These techniques are not secret collusive moves to play off one partner against the other, but encouragements to become more curious about one another. For example, the DP could be asked to hide certain successes or leave certain tasks deliberately undone, or make ritualized statements of distress to the partner at specific times. The partner may be invited to make informed guesses as to what are real and what are simulated episodes. Alternatively, the partner could be invited to pretend, at certain times, that the DP is not depressed and then to respond to the DP on the basis of that assumption, with both encouraged to note when this happens and what the consequences are. These techniques are designed to disrupt habitual assumptions that maintain the patterns of interaction around the depressive symptoms.

- Focusing on positives. Couples in a predominantly conflictual relationship can be asked to list (separately) what they do not want to change about their partner.

Tasks are designed to provide new information, for therapist and clients, rather than being "prescriptions for more adequate living". The act of monitoring and observation can in itself lead to new understanding and to change. While the therapist is interested in feedback about the task, it is important that the couple should not feel blamed for not carrying out the task, or for modifying it, since all the responses to the task are of use to the therapist and couple in gaining more understanding of their patterns of interaction and beliefs. While some specific examples and generic tasks were mentioned above, tasks or rituals essentially emerge from the specific therapist–couple interaction in a particular session and therefore constitute a collaboration rather than a demand by the therapist.

11. Special issues

11a: Gender

- *The gender of the therapist*

  As couple therapy implies a threesome, the therapist needs to be aware of the potential imbalance that his or her gender creates (Jones, 1996). The problems of threesomes and intimacy is always at issue in couple work, whether or not the couple and the therapist are of the same genders and sexualities. In this research project, the study design meant that the therapist would always be of the same gender as one of the couple, and different from the other. This makes it essential for the therapist to address the gender balance in the room overtly and to be alert to the clients' fears and hopes regarding the therapist's potential understanding of his or her dilemmas. It is similarly important for therapists to monitor the ways in which their own ethnic and cultural identity and their age and class may create difficulties of trust for clients (for further discussion, see chapters three and five).

- *The gender of the patient*

  Depression is much more likely to be diagnosed in women, and slightly more women than men were the designated patients in this study (see also the discussion in chapter five). There are numerous reasons for this: for example, the protective nature of marriage for men (studies suggest that more married women than single women or married men receive treatment for physical and mental disorders), maternal depression after child-birth and when at home with small children, differences in male/female styles of expressing stress, differences in the evaluations made by professionals of similar complaints and behaviours when attributed to women or to men, and so on (Jones, 1994; Knudson-Martin, 1997; Ussher & Nicolson, 1992). This imbalance needs to be borne in mind and, if necessary, addressed in therapy so as to counteract gender stereotyping. Gender roles need to be questioned so that both men and women can identify their gendered belief systems in relation to current and past social relationship patterns, and to the meaning and maintenance of the symptom.

• The overt discussion and exploration of gender issues may arise in relation to the following topics:

—men and women's relationships with children and patterns of parenting (e.g. in regard to the stereotype of "absent fathers" and "over-involved mothers")

—violence: the therapist needs to be alert to hints of violence in the couple's narrative and able to ask specific questions about its occurrence, frequency, and context as well as safety issues; the difficulty of addressing these issues within a systemic framework of even-handedness means that therapists often fail to notice or respond adequately to partner violence (Bograd, 1999; Goldner, 1998; Goldner, Penn, Sheinberg, & Walker, 1990; Hamberger, 1997b; Jacobson & Gottman, 1998; Jones, 1998b; Kaufman, 1992); couples where the man is violent towards the woman (the more common pattern) should be helped to achieve a position where he can take responsibility for controlling the expression of his aggression, and she can take responsibility for ensuring her own safety, as a precondition for being able to engage safely in therapy (for further discussion, see chapters three and five)

—emotional expressiveness: the symptom of depression may, for women or men, be a disguised communication about affect that their social learning does not allow them to show (e.g. anger in her case, or vulnerability in his)

—financial implications of change in relationship, particularly as it affects the possibility of separation

—close confiding relationships between women (and their absence in the lives of men) and how these may impact on the couple relationship

—women's and men's working situation

—the use and abuse of power in relationships, and how this ties in with cultural and societal constructions of permissible and non-permissible power use

—the family patterns and traditions of both partners in relation to gender

—the wider social context and its influence on the construction of male and female roles: this will include questions such as those outlined above, as well as the effects of an androcratic culture and perceptions about power and obligation.

11b: *Non-couple sessions*

During the course of couple therapy, it is not unusual for one or both partners to have individual sessions. Mostly such sessions tend to be couple-initiated, where either both partners agree that only one person should attend, or one partner refuses to come to sessions. In the latter case, all efforts would be made to get the partner to return (including by telephone and letter). The therapist may agree to meet with the individual while spelling out that she or he would not be prepared to be party to a secret in relation to the absent partner.

On some occasions, individual sessions may be thera-
pist-initiated: the therapist may decide to split a session,
with one half for each partner. This may be to overcome
a therapeutic impasse, with the beginning and end of the
session conducted with both partners present and with
agreement regarding the above-mentioned rule-blocking
secrets. In such a split session, each partner might, for
example, be encouraged to think of behaviours that might
pleasantly surprise the partner or may use the space to
discuss individual history or dilemmas, with the knowledge of but without the perhaps protective or inhibiting
presence of the partner.

It may, on occasion, be useful to bring other family
members into the sessions, notably (grand-)parents or children. Invitations to other family members might be framed
as useful in order to hear how they see things, or as helpful
in terms of resolving some old issues.

11d: *Separation*

During couple therapy, issues of separation are likely to
surface—perhaps more readily than in treatments that
single out one person only, be that medication, psycho-
analysis, or cognitive therapy. The therapist maintains a
neutral stance in relation to one or both partners' threat
of imminent separation, or to a decision by the partners to
separate. The therapist will, in such a case, consider with
both partners the implications and consequences of an
envisaged separation in some (concrete) detail. However,
it is not the therapist's task to keep a relationship together
at all costs, and in this respect, as in others, the therapist
maintains a neutral stance towards outcome and decisions
taken by the couple. This can be done by using systemic
interviewing techniques, such as circular questioning,
hypothetical future questions, and so on, to enable the
partners to reflect on the relative advantages and disadvantages of staying together or separating.

CHAPTER THREE

Working with depression, I

Elsa Jones

I attempt in this chapter to discuss, by means of clinical examples, some of the ways in which I worked with couples in the study. I look at what I think worked, what I found difficult, where I struggled and failed to help the clients, and what I learned in the process. Clients gave permission for material from the work with them to be used for the research programme, and, where relevant, I renegotiated this permission after the completion of the work; nevertheless, I would like to stress my hope that my treatment of their therapy, and your reading of it, can be done with respect for their privacy, and with gratitude to them for the opportunity to enhance our professional understanding. Pseudonyms are used, biographical and therapeutic accounts are condensed, and identifying details are altered.

The material in this chapter is organized around certain themes and patterns that seem to me central to this work, using detailed examples from the work with one couple and short illustrative anecdotes from other case material. Other themes will be elaborated in chapter five. As pointed out in chapters one and two, the work done with these couples does not constitute a newly invented model of psychotherapy; it is systemic couples therapy done in the context of a comparative research programme.

Depression

I have suggested elsewhere (Jones, 1994) that as a psychotherapist I find it useful to think of depression as a response to the experience of powerlessness, which may have been triggered by childhood and family experiences such as abuse and neglect, by more recent interpersonal experiences such as loss of attachments and relationships, by helplessness before the workings of fate, or loss of the sense of personal agency or potency in the face of contextual accidents or abuses of power, or by combinations of all of these. The well-established links between depression, social isolation, poverty, or unemployment, and the ways in which these are modulated by gender, will interact with individual factors of resilience and personal history to render a certain person, at a certain time, unable to shake off the effects of adversity, and thus vulnerable to being "pressed down". This is not to deny that the complex feedback system of physiology and emotion is relevant here; it is, rather, a question of focusing on those areas amenable to the expertise of this particular approach.

The designated patients with whom I worked in this project had all experienced some or many of the following triggers for depression: physical and sexual abuse in childhood, past and ongoing racism and discrimination, unemployment, infertility, sexual impotence, educational and social marginalization, bereavement, abandonment and the loss of familiar supports, violence and hostility from partners, and the unjust blows of fate or chance. On the one hand, one could say that this litany of suffering is the lot of humankind, and that not everyone who experiences these misfortunes becomes depressed enough to receive a psychiatric diagnosis and, in some cases, years and decades of unsuccessful psychiatric treatment. On the other hand, one could also say, as a therapist, that there is nothing in the repertoire of psychotherapy that can undo these grievous hurts, and thus there is no point in working therapeutically in such circumstances.

However, from a systemic perspective, we may not always be able to affect the structures, events, or other participants in the systems of which we are a part, but we can sometimes shift our dis-position within the system, and thus become re-empowered to change the meaning of our own role. By "dis-position" (Jones, 1998a), I mean where I stand in the system in relation to others, what I stand for and am taken for (my position), as well as my frame of my mind, the way in which I attribute meaning and emotion to my experiences (my disposition). I use the word in a hyphenated form as a reminder of both of these potential meanings, which then allows me to think about what, in my dis-position, might be amenable to change. I might, for example, change where I stand in relation to others in the system in regard to proximity, point of view, alliance, and so on, or I may change my emotional or relational stance towards them. Since I am a part of the observing system within which therapy takes place, change in my dis-position may invite or trigger change for others, and I am more able to change myself than to change others. Such a change in dis-position may then lead to an acceptance of what cannot be changed, and a sense of existential responsibility for how one conducts oneself in the face of, for example, the untimely death of a child; it may also bring about a freedom for greater self-definition, changed responses and demands in relation to others, a sense of self-worth and "agency" in relation to the world "out there", or shifts in the meanings and feelings associated with one's life experiences.

Individual focus or interactional focus?

Because of the research context, we were aware of the necessity of being respectful of the diagnostic status of one of the couple members (see also chapter five); in other words, the partners were not necessarily asking for couple therapy for problems in the relationship, but the "undiagnosed" partner had agreed to accompany the DP to therapy. How important or unimportant this factor was varied from couple to couple. In some situations, the focus remained on the difficulties of one person and the way in which the partner might be able to assist her or him; in other cases, the emphasis switched early on—or even before the first meeting with the therapist—to difficulties experienced within the couple's relationship, which some couples overtly linked to the DP's symptoms.

EXAMPLE

Martin was a 31-year-old white British professional man. His current episode of depression, lasting several years, was seen by him to have been triggered by his becoming infertile following illness, the effects of the fertility treatment he had subsequently undergone in the hope that and his wife Mary might be able to have another child in addition to their 10-year-old son, bullying from his previous boss and the eventual loss of his job, and the severe stress in the marriage. While Martin presented the terrible arguments between himself and Mary, resulting in their living separately, as the main problem currently linked to his depressed feelings, Mary strenuously denied this. From her perspective, the rows were the *consequence* of Martin's depression and lack of confidence, which she saw as a life-long pattern that had merely been aggravated by recent events. She felt blamed and attacked by any attempt to involve her in exploration of interactional patterns or in trying out new behaviours. She said that she was attending the sessions in part because she, like Martin, had some hope that the relationship might be saved for the sake of their child, and in part because she had given up on the relationship but hoped that they could separate amicably. She indicated that she should be treated as at best an observer of the work. Yet Martin felt strongly that, while some of his despair related to his own sense of who he was—and was no longer—his unhappiness was largely situated in the ruin of their relationship. Thus the task for the therapist was to keep Martin engaged in the work by accepting his interactional problem definition, and also to keep Mary engaged by not making her feel blamed by an interactional perspective.

In the early stages of the work, the therapist therefore concentrated on trying to help Martin develop increased self-confidence by means of support, understanding of the personal and contextual antecedents of his depression, and suggestions for new behaviours. Since many of these inevitably had some impact on the relationship with Mary, it was also incumbent on me, as the therapist, to attempt to explore different responses from Mary, without implying that her irritation and contempt were causative in Martin's loss of confidence. One could almost say that the therapy ran on parallel tracks for the first few sessions. The therapist resolutely held onto a systemic "no-blame" stance—that is, the idea that individuals do what they can find to do under the constraints of their experience of their position, over time, in the systems that they co-constitute. This stance eventually reassured Mary that she was not going to be held unilaterally responsible for Martin's frame of mind. This enabled her to begin to claim space for herself in the sessions, talking about the way in which at times she found herself trapped in an "angry mother" style.

EXAMPLE

Anne was a 44-year-old white woman whose psychiatric history dated back some thirty years. She had had numerous hospital admissions for depression and also following suicide attempts. She quoted, with a sort of amused and bemused acceptance, a casualty reception doctor who had said that "suicide had become a way of life for her". She had experienced multiple losses and abuses and, at the time we first met, was living with her 15-year-old son in a council flat, where she spent most days in bed unable to motivate herself to move. Her partner Andrew had been in the relationship with her for more than a year, and therefore technically they qualified for inclusion in the study. However, Andrew lived in a single-men's hostel, and while he was willing to be helpful to Anne where possible, he knew little about her life and was not much involved in her day-to-day existence. About half-way through the therapy, he disappeared for a while—going "walkabout" was apparently part of his usual repertoire—and I continued to meet with Anne alone until Andrew returned. Thus, though he was willing to be supportive, and to attend sessions when he was around, the therapy can best be described as individual work accompanied by a friend.

EXAMPLE

Sometimes a couple focus is intrinsic to the work, not because the relationship between the partners is significantly part of the problem, but because their individual histories and dynamics are such that they have become locked together into a vicious spiral, so that a move from one may entangle the other further, and so on, to the distress of both. A year before starting therapy, Dan, a 55-year-old plumber, had lost the job where he had worked all his adult life, due to the fraud and bankruptcy of his employers. Consequently he had lost his entitlement to redundancy and pension payments and had very little hope of finding employment again. Six months later, two of his younger brothers had died of heart disease within a fortnight of each other; his father had died of similar causes at the age of 59. It is not surprising that Dan was depressed at this point. However, a complicating factor emerged from his wife Dorothy's history. When she was a teenager her father had lost his job, followed by the death of a near relative; he had then become an alcoholic, leading to several years of great family unhappiness before he died—in the psychiatric hospital in which we were meeting! Dorothy's fear that history was about to repeat itself made her extremely anxious about Dan's communications of grief and distress, and Dan's preoccupation with his own experiences meant that he was unable to feel sympathetic towards Dorothy's panic about his depression. In order for "the depression" to change, the system had to unlock itself from its circular and self-reinforcing closed feedback loop.

Getting started

Other couples start therapy with a focus on difficulties in the couple relationship. Thus the therapist can, from the beginning, explore the meaning and context of the DP's depression and the ways in which the couple relationship might interact with this, as aggravation, trigger, or maintenance. By focusing on the regularities of feedback and pattern within the relationship, as well as on individual contexts and constructions of meaning, the likelihood of lasting change for all those involved in the therapy is enhanced. Indeed, change is also likely to reach out and affect those not present in the therapy room, but meaningfully interlinked with the changing couple system, and the partners can support each other in attempting changed interactions. This makes it much more likely that the therapeutic work will be continued in the periods between sessions, which anchors the work and ensuing change more in the ownership of the couple than in the fiefdom of the therapist.

EXAMPLE

Kathy, a white Englishwoman aged 29, had been physically and sexually abused in childhood, had been abandoned by her mother at the age of 6 years, and had spent some years in childhood involved in delinquency, ending up with a period in local authority care. She had undergone a forced abortion after being raped in early adolescence, and she experienced herself throughout these events as passive and voiceless, with others acting upon her and on her behalf. She had one younger brother, who was said to be brain-damaged because of being kicked in the head repeatedly by both parents in childhood. Her first partner, the father of her 11-year-old daughter Tracy, had been physically violent towards her, as was her current partner Ken, with whom she had a 2-year-old daughter, Ally. She was not currently employed.

Although Kathy had repeatedly been diagnosed as depressed since she was 14, and had received a great deal of medication and some counselling, all without effect, the central topic that she wanted to table at the start of therapy was her poor relationship with Ken and her own sense of worthlessness.

Kathy arrived alone for the first session, saying that Ken was due to come straight from work, although she thought it possible that he might not arrive, as he had been very anxious and was only attending because of her threat to leave him if he did not join her in attempts to change their situation. As she had threatened to leave him before, and had done so once or twice, it was not clear how effective a threat this might be at present. My experience of couples work generally is that it is not uncommon for one partner (often the man) to attend initially under coercion, and it is then the therapist's task to establish something resembling a level playing field, where both partners can have the confidence that they will be treated equitably.

Because of Ken's absence at the start of the session, I asked Kathy to ensure that we did not discuss material that would make it harder for him to join us at a later stage; this means that I blocked attempts to discuss their difficulties as a couple, and I concentrated on a detailed exploration of Kathy's family history and the history of her involvement with mental health professionals. Ken did arrive about two-thirds of the way through the session, smelling of beer. I decided to treat this as an example of Dutch courage, although well aware of the inadvisability, in general, of working with clients under the influence of alcohol. Having explained to Ken what Kathy and I had been discussing, I then invited him also to discuss his family background. This information, and the degree of engagement that ensued with both of them because of having heard, with interest, their accounts of sad and difficult circumstances, proved invaluable in the second session when we had to deal urgently with the dilemma of violence. It is in any case usual for systemic therapists to obtain multi-generational information near the beginning of a piece of work. This establishes a sense of the contexts within which clients have acquired their beliefs and patterns about roles and identities, and it acts as a signal to the clients about the therapist's style, and areas of curiosity.

Ken, also white and English, was the youngest of three children. His father drank and regularly assaulted his mother, who "for the sake of the children" remained with the father until Ken was 16. In childhood, Ken felt sympathy for his mother and anger towards his father, but when his mother left, offering him a home with herself and her new partner, he stayed because of the hope for closeness kindled in him by observing his father's emotional collapse. However, two years later he gave up any hope of nurturing from his father, having experienced hunger and continued neglect. He worked now as an unskilled builder's labourer. (It will be obvious that both Kathy and Ken belong to what is usually called the working class. I find myself, as an incomer to British class culture, increasingly uncomfortable with using the usual class designations, partly because they seem to me so crucial and loaded in their designations of identity, and partly because I cannot help hearing the irony in the phrase "working class" for those most often vulnerable to unemployment. I will therefore leave readers to draw their own conclusions about class from my descriptions.) The relationship with Kathy was for Ken the first serious one. He was very keen that it should be made to work, but anxious and defensive about the possibility of being blamed.

The work with Kathy and Ken is used to explore the main themes of this chapter.

Crises and safety

Following the first session there was a considerable gap before the next session, partly because they cancelled two appointments because of crises to do with Ken's job, and partly because Christmas intervened. During the second session, they told me that they had had a major row on Christmas Eve, resulting in Ken assaulting Kathy. Kathy had also in the interval seen a child guidance worker in relation to Tracy, who had signalled at school that she was very unhappy about the situation at home. The worker had told Kathy that she should leave Ken, which had left her feeling "stupid" and misunderstood. The session was spent getting a detailed breakdown of the violent incident and working towards a "safety contract" with them.

There is a considerable body of writing on the ideas and techniques involved in work with couples where one partner is violent towards the other (Bograd, 1999; Dobash & Dobash, 1992; Geffner, 1997; Goldner, 1998; Goldner et al., 1990; Jacobson & Gottman, 1998; Jasinski & Williams, 1998; Jones, 1998b). I will not here go into detail except to summarize the highlights. Firstly, it is useful to make a distinction between "mutual combat" and battering: where we are talking of battering, the size, power, and sense of entitlement of one partner contrasts with the sense of paralysis, intimidation, depression, and fear of the other, even if both engage in physical attack (Hamberger, 1997a; Jacobson & Gottman, 1998). It is often to be observed that couples in a relationship where the man batters the woman find themselves unable to separate; indeed, for both of them the failure to separate and the rewards of reconciliation after violence may constitute the deepest meaning of the relationship. Additionally, each may hold the other responsible in a strange symmetry that continues to leave the pattern of violence uninterrupted. That is, the woman feels that the man should be responsible for rendering her safe: "if only he loved me enough he would not hurt me . . ."; thus, she is unwilling to remove herself and her children to safety when she realizes that a situation is escalating towards violence. He also holds her responsible for his violence: "If only she didn't provoke me. . . ." Thus, he does not take responsibility for how he expresses his anger, frustration, or whatever emotional arousal acts for him as the trigger to his violence.

Kathy and Ken fitted this pattern: Kathy felt that it was unfair that she should be expected to safeguard herself, since it was Ken who was in the wrong; Ken felt that she "made him do it". However, for the therapist it is vital to discover whether the couple can begin to show interest in this new division of responsibility, often expressed as the therapist's need to have a safe basis for future work. Unless such a baseline is reached, further work may indeed involve the therapist in collusion which results in the further battering of one partner by the other. The art of the work consists in indicating at one and the same time two perspectives: that is, the therapist requires a lineal acknowledgement of the unacceptability of violence, whatever the perceived provocation, and she also indicates her wide-ranging non-judgemental interest in the antecedents, contexts, and relational feedback loops surrounding the act of violence. By the end of this second session, Kathy and Ken had each expressed a commitment to trying this new way of dealing with their rows and frustrations.

In hearing a description of the violent incident, I attempted especially to invite Ken to give his own account of what he had done, as well as the events that led up to it. This served to place him in a position of responsibility as someone owning the narrative of his actions, and it avoided the "prisoner-in-the-dock" phenomenon likely if the therapist had allowed Kathy to do most of the initial talking about Ken's actions. What was striking about Ken's account was the passivity of his view of himself. His narrative was studded with phrases like "I couldn't help it", "they made me do it" (his mates who had inveigled him into a drinking spree so that he abandoned the planned Christmas outing with Kathy), "I had to hit her", "It wasn't my fault" . This enabled me, knowing from previous discussion how important his image of himself as a masculine man was, to invite him to engage in therapy as a means of finding a way to be more in control of his life.

Establishing a shared therapeutic agenda

Kathy's account of her perceptions of the incident and what led up to it provided a vivid view of her low sense of self-worth: "They think I'm not good enough for them", "He thought he could just dump me there", " My plans count for nothing". This low self-esteem is closely intertwined with her depression, and it triggered her feeling of rejection and worthlessness on the Christmas morning when Ken finally arrived home.

A further aggravation of the situation derives from Kathy's sense, from earliest childhood, that whenever there is a triangle in relationships she will be the one to be pushed out. This applies particularly to her experiences in childhood of her abandonment by her mother, of the excluding closeness between her father and step-mother after her mother's departure and to her experiences with her first husband's infidelities and her hurt about Ken's one-night stand while she was giving birth to Ally. She identifies this, as the therapeutic work continues, as one of the reasons why she cannot let go of the relationship even though she is at risk of serious harm and has tried to leave Ken in the past; she does not believe that Ken loves her now, but sees herself as merely being tolerated as Ally's mother. In other words, she is again the barely tolerated outsider in the relationship that Ken has with his daughter, and so she feels obliged to cling on.

Ken is similarly trapped in a sense that the relationship cannot work, and yet he is unable to leave: he is deeply jealous of Kathy's relationship with Tracy's father, and with Tracy herself, and believes that Kathy cannot care for him now because he has behaved so badly towards her. He believes that she stays with him only because he has frightened her with his threats of what he might do if she leaves, and thus can derive no comfort from her presence in the relationship, while being unable to let her go. He has recently observed that Ally seems to be afraid of him, and this becomes a strong motivation for his continuing participation in the hard work of change, since in Ally he sees his own childhood self and realizes that, despite his best intentions, he has become like his violent drunken father.

Patterns from the past in the present

For both partners, exploration of patterns learned in the past became a significant feature of their attempts to change current unhelpful patterns of interaction between the two of them and with others. Kathy found the idea of repeating triangles extremely useful and started observing her responses to "outsider" experiences. The sense that her repeated experiences of being abused in relationships might have something to do with learned expectations, the behaviour of others as well as herself, and contexts beyond her control allowed her to begin to shed the sense of herself as someone who deserved little or who "asked for" abuse.

During the therapy she became involved in a retraining programme for mothers of young children intending to return to
work, and she found the assertiveness training that formed
part of the package very useful. By bringing this new learning
into the therapy sessions, she was able to test out and integrate
her new skills and explore her burgeoning sense of herself as
someone who, despite grave setbacks, had nevertheless man-
aged to reach adulthood able to love and be loved, and as
worthy of more than she had put up with to date. As she stood
up for herself more, she of course received new, different, and
more rewarding feedback from most people, which encouraged her to experiment with a wider repertoire of self-expres-
sion.

It was also important here that the therapist did not shame
Kathy in respect of her failure to leave Ken. The regular experience
of women in Kathy's position is that well-meaning and concerned
people tell them that they must leave their violent partners. Their
failure to do so may rest on a complexity of factors, such as lack of
money, resources, and alternatives, social conditioning, intimidation, family and gendered learning about expectations and role, or
love and protectiveness towards their partner. However, this
leaves them feeling to blame if they remain with a violent partner,
or return to him after attempted separation. This was Kathy's experience of being "made to feel stupid" by previous counsellors.
As Virginia Goldner has reminded us (Goldner et al., 1990), it can
be hard for therapists to acknowledge that women may love men
who hurt them. Our failure to extricate them from such relationships often make us turn on them with pejorative theories about,
for example, "female masochism".

It was equally important for the therapist not to shame Ken
because of his continuing loyalty to his father. We therefore explored the ways in which Ken wished to be different from his
father, and we hoped that Ally would not, twenty years hence,
have to have conversations with a therapist about the ways in
which her father had brutalized her mother. At the same time we
looked at the ways in which Ken cared for and about his father
and valued some of the traditional masculine activities, like foot-

ball matches and playing cards, which they shared. Ken gradually became aware that he had no models for masculine behaviour which did not involve violence and emotional and relational inarticulateness.

Talking about gender

In a sense, Ken and Kathy embody the extremes of the generally accepted gender stereotypes. Ken earns his living by virtue of his physical strength, is emotionally inarticulate (Frosh, 1992), resorts to violence under circumstances where he feels afraid, out of control, or uncertain (e.g. when he fears that he will lose Kathy), resorts to action rather than speech, and is emotionally disconnected from others (Taffel, 1991). Kathy is emotionally expressive along the vulnerability/softness continuum but is unable to assert herself effectively; she does not feel any sense of entitlement or self-worth, and she assumes that her lot in life is to be passive and victimized, and to look after others without expecting much for herself, while still yearning to be loved as a way of validating her life.

In the course of the therapeutic work, we explored the ways in which they had learned gender, and might re-learn it, in a variety of direct and indirect ways. The therapist's own gender and age was obviously relevant here: Kathy clearly took certain aspects of my behaviour and speech on board as models of potentially different options for herself. It is useful for therapists of whichever gender to remember that we are more androgynous, in the eyes of clients, than we might sometimes think (Jones, 1993). In this way we might offer models of assertive "masculine" speech and demeanour that women clients might find useful, but also of listening and empathic "feminine" skills that male clients might find more accessible when coming from someone other than a partner. Nevertheless, when working with a heterosexual couple, the therapist's perceived gender can act as an unbalancing factor. I was therefore alert to the possibility that Ken might at times feel "outnumbered", and I therefore brought male "voices" into the therapy via anecdotes or information from and about men.

As Ken continued his search for a different way to be a man, I offered him information, in language and format that fitted with his situation, about the current awareness of, and struggle with, the dilemmas that have been called "the crisis of masculinity" in contemporary society. It was useful for him to learn that he was not alone in his attempts to chart unexplored territory. One example may give the flavour of many small interactions and anecdotes.

Ken and Kathy had begun to explore small ways of changing their relationship by means of inter-session tasks, which were planned in the sessions by all of us, and emerged from their current situation. Kathy had said that she longed for more conversation between them. For example, when Ken came home from work she would like more than a grunt when asking him about his day, and would like him to ask about hers. Kathy, at such a point, is in the situation familiar to housewives with young children, of having spent the day without adult conversation. Ken, on the other hand, having returned from an exhausting and dispiriting day of physical labour, wants only to slump in front of the TV, have his tea, and go to sleep. However, he agreed to try. At the next session, Kathy reported, with much amusement, that Ken had dutifully enquired about her day; she had embarked on an anecdote about a run-in with the greengrocer—and then had to restrain Ken by grabbing the back of his belt as he was running out of the room to go and beat up the greengrocer. This then evolved into a discussion about the possibility of expressing support not by action and problem-solving, but by merely listening empathically. Ken was quite sceptical about the thought that mere talking, sharing feelings, and so on might be useful.

The risk in pursuing this line was that Kathy and I, as women, would become experts on something that Ken, as a man, lacked. I therefore told him, in considerable dramatic detail, the story recounted by Brian Dimmock (Reimers & Dimmock, 1990) about his own struggle with this self-same dilemma, in which his attempts to stop his child's distress via problem-solving, reasonableness, and so on fail, whereas his empathic admission of shared feelings is helpful to her (and to him). Ken was riveted by the story. It seems to me that it fulfilled several functions: it offered an example or model of a different way in which a man might behave in a situation where the search for closure and problem-solution is not helpful, and the modelling derived from a man who was a colleague of the therapist (i.e. someone who, within the therapeutic context is seen to have power and status) and, moreover, an educated man who writes articles for professional journals. Thus it becomes possible for Ken to join other men in their exploration of the "crisis of masculinity" and therefore to feel honoured for this, rather than humiliated.

Curiosity and a self-observing stance

The therapist's techniques of circular questioning, of exploring and sharing hypotheses, and of constantly implying the possibility of multiple descriptions act as invitations to clients to become curious about their own patterns of behaviour, emotion, and relationship. This is probably one of the linchpins in the bringing about of change in systemic therapy. There are also more direct actions on the therapist's part that allow a client, for a period, to enter a position in which they can observe rather than participate.

> For example, in the fifth session Kathy spoke of a telephone discussion she had had with a friend of Ken's in which she had stood her ground and had explained her views about his drunken escapades with Ken and the ways in which he tended to discount her. She felt very pleased with her own assertiveness and felt that she had reached a good and respectful agreement with the friend. Ken, however, was alarmed and furious, and he started interrupting Kathy's account of the conversation to the therapist with increasingly aggressive remarks. He stated that Kathy had no right to talk to his friend behind his back, and his continuous interruptions, tone of voice, and body posture became intimidating to Kathy, who started veering between being apologetic and enraged. To me it looked like the sort of interaction that, had they been at home, might well have

escalated into violence. I therefore started interrupting Ken's interruptions by repeatedly saying, in an escalating tone of voice: "Is this how you intimidate her?" (referring to Ken's account, previously, of the ways in which he intimidates Kathy in order to ensure that she will be too frightened to leave him). Eventually my behaviour irritated Ken sufficiently that he turned from Kathy to me and continued vehemently to argue his view that Kathy should never interact with other men. Our conversation escalated for a while and then subsided into a more cooperative tone.

The components of this process were, in my view, as follows: I challenged Ken from a position of confidence and lack of fear, due to my professional experience and role and the setting in which we were meeting, so that I was not giving out signals of anxiety in the way that Kathy might have done. I also relied on my gender and age, our already-established relationship, and my knowledge of his affection for and protectiveness towards his mother, enabling me to make use of the fact that I was of the same generation as she was. As I have said elsewhere (Jones, 1996), different therapists (black, male, or young, for example) will have to access other parts of the shared repertoire with clients in order to carry out similar risky actions. I also, when it seemed safe, invoked humour, having already found that this was something I could share with them. Thus, when Ken said at a certain point, "But she knows she musn't do such things Elsa, because she knows if she does I have to hit her", I could say, with some camaraderie, "Oh, come off it, Ken— you know by now I don't fall for that sort of argument": the result was his rueful laughter. In the process of this interaction, Ken was invited repeatedly by me to observe his current behaviour and connect it to previous, more thoughtful, exploration of his patterns of vulnerability. Thus, towards the end of this episode, I could increasingly use words like "afraid", "lost", and "jealous" in place of his offered words of territorial control and anger, and he could increasingly accept them.

Kathy, on the other hand, had the opportunity to stand back from a challenging escalating situation in which she is usually a participant, and she could therefore observe the usual patterns— which she would normally be too agitated to note—and could also take note of the ways in which my interactions with Ken were different from, and perhaps more effective than, her previous responses.

Reframing

Following the incident above, Ken started talking about an observation he had made about the difference between himself and Kathy. He said to the therapist: "You must think I'm stupid because you keep asking questions like 'what do you think?', 'What's your point of view?', and so on, and I keep saying 'I don't know'." He went on to explain that this was not because he was uncooperative, but because, as far as he was concerned, he had no inner life. This had particularly been the case since Ally's birth, when he had for a period been afraid that he might have picked up a sexually transmitted illness from his sexual adventure at the time; this led him to confess to Kathy. He had continued since then to feel listless, exhausted, and what he called "lazy". As I explored this in detail with him, Kathy became more and more fascinated, until she eventually said: "But he's depressed, just like I was."

I was reminded of Taffel's view that ". . . the distinction between depression and the everyday state of many men is not so clearcut. What should we call someone who does not feel very much, who has no real friendships, who has few interests other than work, and who cannot relate to the people close at hand?" (Taffel, 1991, p. 258). Framing Ken's state of mind as depression was, in this context, experienced as positive because Kathy had been depressed for many years and was, by this stage, already becoming significantly un-depressed; that is, in their experience depression was something now from which it was possible to recover. It also allowed Kathy to become more sympathetic and supportive towards Ken, and for Ken to accept some overt "coaching" from Kathy in relation to her being further along the "recovery route" than he was.

Homework

The creation of tasks and rituals for clients to perform at home has always been part of the family therapy repertoire. By doing work at home—whether an observation task, an experiment with intermittent new behaviour, or a ritual of healing or paradoxical intent—the loop created between the boundaried space of the therapy encounter and the intricacies of the clients' everyday lives is an important one. Homework tasks not only produce information for therapist and clients; they also situate change behaviour and meaning attribution in such a way that the client is likely to have a greater sense of ownership and autonomy in relation to whatever emerges. Ideally homework gets constructed out of the ideas generated cooperatively within the session.

> Kathy and Ken used homework tasks to try out new ways of relating to each other and to others, and they would then bring their observations from these to the sessions for discussion and further unpacking. In this way they started experimenting with different ways of spending time with the children and with friends. Kathy had previously tried to keep her relationship with Tracy almost hidden from Ken, for fear that his negative responses might make things worse for her daughter. Now she began to spend "quality time" with Tracy, partly as a normal mother–daughter activity, and partly in response to Tracy's distress that had earlier alerted the educational services. At the same time, Ken also began to forge an independent relationship with Tracy, and Kathy, with some trepidation, stepped aside to allow them to do this. These efforts happened within the context of new self-awareness, and also fostered more self-knowledge and self-observation. They told me of an occasion when Kathy had arranged for Ally to spend the day with Ken's mother so that she and Tracy could have a "girl's day out". This had gone very well, and they arrived home, in high good humour, about five minutes after Ken, to find him scowling and demanding to know where they had been. Instead of her previously usual sense of having got things wrong, which would then have triggered a placatory, anxious, defensive response, Kathy interpreted his stance as meaning that his nose

was somewhat out of joint (because she had been out with her daughter instead of at home cooking his meal). She laughed, put her arms around him, and said: "I have been thinking about you, I've got us a take-away." Ken could then also respond with self-awareness and humour.

Humour

Humour is, as Bateson (1972) reminds us, a trans-contextual syndrome; that is, it leaps across boundaries, allows disparate contexts and learning levels to be put together, and is therefore closely linked to the mechanisms of change and creativity. Or, to put it more simply, it is difficult to be rigid when you're laughing. I have a fondness for the absurd, and I make small forays from the beginning of my contact with new clients to see whether this might also be the case with them. One must, of course, be careful not to cause offence by seeking for laughter in tragic circumstances, but information that suggests that clients might be able to use humour acts as a great encouragement to me.

> Ken and Kathy had given early signs of being able to laugh in the midst of distress, and this developed as they began to feel more free and confident. In their negotiations about change, Kathy had voiced her objections about Ken's weekly poker match with his father and other cronies, which Ken was unwilling to give up. He also had not been willing to telephone her if he thought he might be unusually late. For Kathy, a late-night vigil waiting for Ken tended to trigger her worst fears: that Ken might be with another woman, or that he would come home drunk and beat her up. After some negotiation, she agreed that she could accept his night out "with the boys" and, in return, would also have "a night out with the girls", going clubbing, since she liked to dance and Ken did not. This discussion happened in the context of the therapist suggesting that they might consider going out together, which they labelled as middle-class and bizarre!
>
> The feedback on this experiment was given by Ken with a great deal of self-deprecating laughter. On about Kathy's third out-

ing, she had not come home at the time expected, when the clubs closed, and nor had she telephoned. Ken became anxious, convinced that she had gone off with another man. He then described his anxious time of alternately checking that the children were asleep, then going around the dark streets on his bicycle checking various other possible venues, each time returning to check on the children. "There I was, riding through the dark like a fool, very scared and also laughing my head off because I looked so silly." This was a very different stance from his earlier striving for control and dominance. Having now experienced the anxiety both ways, they could agree a system of giving responsible messages to allay the other's fears.

Choice and the anticipation of the future

In later sessions, the focus of the therapy begins to shift towards anticipation and fantasy rehearsal of the future. With this comes a sense of having some choices within the constraints of context and circumstance.

Quite early on, as Kathy became less depressed and more overtly angry, she said firmly that she would no longer accept the conditions that had obtained previously in her relationship with Ken and with her previous partner. She knew that on her own, with two children and no formal education, she would face severe poverty, but she also no longer believed that she had to accept abuse and neglect for the sake of remaining in a relationship.

At a later stage, Ken said that although they were not yet sure that they would be able to stay together, because of the legacy of past actions, they had been talking about their realization that, even if they split up, they would be highly unlikely to make similar destructive relationships again. Kathy's changed self-perceptions also impinged on her ways of relating to her daughters and would clearly offer them a different model of how to be a woman. Through the training course she started, Kathy began to make new friends, and by the end of therapy she had started a business from home together with a friend, which in turn impacted on her self-esteem and on the family's financial situation.

Both partners were required to complete the Beck Depression Inventory at regular intervals, and many clients in the project used this also as an ongoing way of monitoring their own progress.

Ken pointed out to me, about half-way through the therapy, that he was beginning to "get a score" on the BDI. That is, while initially he had been so cut off from any sense of self-awareness that he had simply answered "no" to all questions, he was now recording, in particular, his sense of sadness about his loneliness. He said that he had noticed how Kathy talked with her friends and also with me and with his mother, and he had watched men in public places and on television and had begun to notice a quality of friendly, confiding relationship that he had never experienced. His "mates" were the men he worked and drank with, and they did not speak to each other in the ways he was now beginning to want. Yet he felt acutely aware of a lack of skills in this regard. However, he was also aware that his capacity to experience and express his sadness about this was an indication of the great journey of change that he was embarking on, with hope for the future. Rachel Hare-Mustin (1998) says: "When we impose an ideal of masculinity on men, we are imposing prescriptions that are often contradictory, such as ideas of men's entitlement juxtaposed with men's sense of inadequacy in meeting what are, after all, impossible goals" (p. 44). As Ken started to give up the idea that he could or should control others, he began to open himself up to learning, feeling, receiving, and changing.

At the conclusion of the therapy we spent part of the session in one-to-one meetings between each of them and myself, thus making a symmetrical pattern with the start of our meetings. This served to underline the sense of their greater autonomy, as well as the acknowledgement that, while the future looked hopeful for them as a couple, the true concern of the therapy was not whether or not they would stay together, but the emotional welfare of each of them (even though the focus of the research project was Kathy's recovery from depression).

> Separately and together, they expressed the view that, while they had both changed significantly, within themselves and in their relationships with each other and with both children, they were not yet sure whether this would mean a future for them as a couple. What was significant was that both now accepted fully the idea that Kathy had choice—that is, that she was not the victim of her life, but the "agent" of it. This meant, for Ken, that he had also taken the frightening step of letting go his grip of her, so that if she remained with him it would be from choice.

Since I hold the view that the experience of powerlessness is central to the cluster of phenomena we call depression, I then also take the gaining of a sense of choice as an indication of the client's sense of empowerment. Thus, for me, this feedback was crucial; however, it was also good to discover, at the end of the two-year follow-up, that Kathy was still free of depression.

Summary

I shall attempt, in order to draw together this long case example, to summarize the useful or significant components of the change process. I do this with some trepidation, since any such attempt must be a subjective punctuation dictated by the partial perspective of the moment. Nevertheless, I hope that it may act as a useful stimulant to readers.

It was possible to create a safe and contained "space" in which risks and changes could be explored; essential to this safety was the fact that I attended with great seriousness to their information about violence and expected each of them to make a commitment that would make future violence less likely. In doing so they were able to signify that they were willing to take responsibility for themselves as individuals, with hope of change for themselves, and as a couple hoping for a future together. We attended to the way that patterns from the past organized their present in such a way that they felt stuck and doomed to endless repetition. By exploring their gender learning and patterning, they were able to get access to a wider repertoire of behaviours. The therapist's style of conversation and questioning is such that clients are continuously invited, overtly and subtly, to consider their statements as representing a point of view amongst many other potential perspectives and, as time goes on, to become curious about their own points of view, beliefs, and so on, so that they become able to take up an observing stance in relation to themselves. We searched together for more positive framings of their dilemmas and devised tasks and experiments that they could carry out in the intervals between sessions, thus ensuring that they were actively involved in bringing about change and expansion in their range of options. They found ways of expressing intense and challenging emotions and points of view without these leading to untenable conflict; this process was helped by the permission to be humorous, even about difficult topics.

Kathy became able, through revisiting her past with the therapist, to attribute different meanings to some of her experiences, and therefore to construct a different view of herself in the present. This gave her a greater sense of having an ability to act as someone of worth. These new actions, which demanded and received more respect, received feedback that reinforced her sense of worth and allowed her to experiment further with new ways of being. These changes were explored between Kathy and the therapist, and between her and many other people in her life, but most importantly also in the presence of and in interaction with Ken, who was on a similar journey of change for himself and in relation to Kathy. Ken's decision to take control of his violent behaviour allowed him to begin to face his own sense of passivity and worthlessness, and to accept and earn the respect implied in the therapist's assumption that he could change. As with Kathy, new actions for Ken led to new rewarding feedback, which allowed him to experiment with further change—for example, with regard to his awareness of his own emotions and vulnerabilities. Thus, together and separately they began to feel that they were no longer tied helplessly to repeating the patterns of the past, but, instead, had some choices about the future.

The "self" of the therapist in the therapeutic relationship

The therapist as part of the problem: trust

I have discussed above ways in which the therapist can use aspects of her own perceived identity, such as age, class, or gender, to make a certain impact in the work with clients. There are also times when attributes of the therapist can constitute an obstacle to the work and will, unless addressed, militate against the establishment of trust and cooperation. In such cases it is very much the *therapist's* responsibility to invite discussion of the obstacles. A prime example of such a situation occurs when the therapist is white, as I am, and the client(s) black. This means, in a British context, that the therapist represents a dominant majority, and that it is likely that the clients will have experienced discrimination and racism from representatives of the therapist's ethnic group. Given the often abusive experience of membership of a minority group, and given the power dynamics of the therapy situation, clients will not themselves feel free to discuss issues of racism, which may be directly relevant to the difficulties bringing them to therapy and to their relationship with the therapist. The therapist therefore needs to act overtly and, in all the subtle nuances of communication, in such a way as to make this discussion possible (*Context*, 1999; Miller & Thomas, 1994).

EXAMPLE

Derek, a black Afro-Caribbean man, had returned to London at the age of 7 years with his father and siblings, having spent most of his earlier years on the Caribbean island of his parents' birth. He had started his schooling there, and had enjoyed it, so that his first day in a British school was a considerable shock. He was racially abused by a white classmate during the first school break, slapped her, was excluded from school, and beaten with a whip by his father. It was only after several sessions, during which the therapist had offered many openings to discuss the question of racist experience and the implications of her own whiteness, that this anecdote could be told.

This then led to the disclosure of many other similar experiences, including his own verbal and physical assaults by teachers in the remand school where he was later placed. The careful exploration of these matters, which included the therapist's attempts to indicate her awareness of, and willingness to be held responsible for, the attitudes of white society, provided a context for the discussion of other painful aspects of Derek's life. His father's extreme violence towards him and the rest of the family, and his own violence, in adulthood, towards his wife, Dawn, who had herself experienced many other instances of racial and sexual verbal and physical abuse, became part of the large tapestry of the different ways in which power and powerlessness may be exploited. The therapist's ethnicity, and her acknowledgement of what this might signify to Derek and Dawn, placed her inside this tapestry, not outside, and facilitated the thoughtful discussion of victimization and aggression.

EXAMPLE

Salman (aged 34) and Safia (aged 17) were an Indian couple who had both grown up in a Francophone country far from Britain, and they had married in that country, via family arrangement, the previous year. Salman's depression was caused by failure to consummate the marriage, due to his erectile impotence. There were many factors relevant to the triggering and maintenance of Salman's depression and Safia's—perhaps equal—distress, such as the role played by both their families of origin, Safia's youth and loneliness, their relative lack of sexual knowledge, and so on, but these could not be addressed properly until the obstacles to the therapeutic relationship became more available for discussion. Again, the therapist repeatedly invited the clients to a consideration of these, which included an acknowledgement of the limitations to their choice of helper. It was clear that their poverty and the catchment area they lived in meant that they were unlikely to receive good therapeutic help outside the research project. I wondered whether they should transfer to the other systemic therapist, thinking that Salman, as a Muslim man, might find it easier to discuss sexual difficulties with a male doctor. However, for Salman, my gender was not the primary obstacle to working together. Far more important, for him, was the "Western" identity package he attributed to me; he was clear that he would make similar assumptions about Eia. He had had negative experiences with other (male) medical professionals he had previously approached for help. He assumed that I (and Eia) would endorse Western values such as feminism, sexually decadent social customs, materialism, and Christianity. He was very critical of these, and he attempted to protect Safia against these corrupting influences, since she was considerably younger than him, less fluent in English, and new to Britain where he had lived for about ten years. However, these protective impulses had also become entangled with the difficulties between them, so that the less competent he felt as a man, the more he tried to control her; the lonelier and more isolated she became, the more she looked to him for love, sexual gratification, and a baby to keep her company.

I did not try to confirm or deny the assumptions that Salman held about my values (some would fit, others not). Instead, I encouraged discussion of these, and of their different beliefs and values. I conducted bits of the sessions in (poor) French, so as to allow them (and especially Safia) the experience of superiority in their own fluency in their first language. I repeatedly contextualized my opinions as deriving from my (biased) position. For example, I talked with them about my view that their sexual inexperience and lack of information, combined with the high excitement, exhaustion, and sexual innuendo of the wedding ceremony, which stretched over several days, meant that a failure to perform on Salman's part was hardly surprising. However, he maintained that no one else in his circumstances had ever failed, and therefore the fault lay with him. We debated this issue in many ways and forms, always with an overt contextualizing of my opinions as coming from a Western, and therefore potentially prejudiced, position. In time, these debates were accompanied with much fondness, laughter, challenge, and curiosity about different cultural customs; it became possible for me to impart quite a bit of sexual information, and some classic sexual desensitization techniques, which they used creatively and happily, in the guise of "this is how we weird Westerners might go about it".

The therapist as part of the problem: getting stuck

EXAMPLE

Lorna (the DP) and Larry, white, both in their mid-30s, were among the first couples I started seeing in the depression study, and among the ones who benefited least. There are probably many factors accounting for this, and it may be that it would have been difficult to help them in any context.

Contributions to stuckness from their side of the system are manifold: Lorna had been violently assaulted by her alcoholic mother throughout her childhood, and these assaults continued into the present; this shaped her desperate desire to believe that people might become "nice" if only one kept hoping and holding onto them. Lorna and Larry had been together about four years, during which they had lived a chaotic and desperate life in several cities and countries: they had lived rough on the streets, in squats, and in homeless accommodation, during which time Lorna had aborted the child she was expecting, as she felt her slender survival resources would be stretched beyond breaking by the presence of an infant. Lorna had briefly been employed but had lost this job due to her depression; she had put her invalidity money into a business project of Larry's, which later failed. They had both taken great risks with careless drug use and sex, so that both were undergoing tests in relation to HIV status when therapy started. Considerable violence played a regular part in their relationship, and neither acknowledged this as significant. They frequently broke up and then made up the relationship, and Larry was, most of the time, also involved in sexual relationships with other women.

My contribution to the stuckness seems to me, in retrospect, to be linked to my entry into the research project. I had come from fifteen years of working only in teams, so that the new experience of working alone with clients without regular consultation with someone sharing my (Milan) orientation was disconcerting. Although Eia and I repeatedly assured each other that we need not be organized by the research context, and that we should feel free to let clinical considerations outweigh any others, I was, of course, strongly influenced by the sense of scrutiny and competition. It is likely that this was at its strongest in the early stages of the project while I was finding my feet in what for me was a strange context. Because I was not based in London, where the study took place, I saw clients in two different venues (one of which was not safe, welcoming, or suited to clinical work) on opposite sides of the great divide of the Thames, travelling by public transport, and working unsociable hours. Thus I spent the early part of the study struggling to establish a sense of security and belonging for myself. While it did not seem to impact on the work with other couples seen early on in the study, there was probably too much mirroring of process between myself and this couple: Lorna and Larry, in their separate experiences of childhood, and in the pattern of their relationship with each other, felt dispossessed, homeless, and without a stable base, and so did I.

Furthermore, in my desire to keep them in therapy for the sake of the study, I broke one of my own cardinal rules in relation to violence in therapy. It was difficult to get clear information about violence, and for a long time, whenever the topic became unavoidable, they both assured me that "their" violence was mutual and trivial. It was only by Session 11 that I began to get a sense of just how serious and frequent Larry's assaults on Lorna were. Although I was familiar with this kind of situation, and knew that their mutual denial of the seriousness of the assaults and their joint fudging of the question of responsibility meant that couple therapy could not successfully and safely be done, I persisted. I knew at this point that the study was having difficulty in recruiting enough patients, I was hooked on not giving up, and thus enacted (again of course with the perfect

20:20 vision of hindsight) another aspect of the client system: like Lorna, I became over-optimistic and determined to prove that persistence could make everything "be nice".

It is also interesting to note that this is my longest piece of work in the study (in number of sessions) and the fattest (in number of supportive letters written, other professionals pulled in, and so on). Had I been working in another context I might have recognized earlier that repetitively doing more of the same was unlikely to be useful; I might also have used the recognition of mirroring and parallel process as an opportunity to understand the system better, and to shift my dis-position within it, which might just, in turn, have led to a more useful outcome for Lorna and Larry.

Idiosyncrasies and exceptions

When psychotherapists gather informally, the talk sometimes turns to the anecdotes that seldom get into print, and to the speculation that, if only we dared to admit what we do when we depart from the manual, these accounts might also be useful or even creative. In this spirit I will confess to an "instructive" interaction with Rosa and Rube.

EXAMPLE

They were exceptional from the word go, in that the study initially had intended a cut-off point at an upper age limit of 65. Rosa, the DP, was 72 and her husband Rube was 92. A Jewish couple, they had lived all their lives in a part of London's East End, where they were surrounded by a supportive and stimulating familiar community. Things had started going downhill when, after Rube's retirement in his 70s, they chose to buy into a retirement home south of the river. Over the years the value of Rube's pension had diminished to the extent that it was difficult for them to travel to visit their old community, or to pursue the active social life they had enjoyed in the past; in addition, many of their friends, old neighbours, and family had died. They had become increasingly isolated, and Rosa became agitated and depressed after the deaths of two of her brothers left her feeling that death was also standing at her door. For both of them, as for many other Jews of their generations, the loss of relatives and friends had added poignancy because of the legacy of the Holocaust. By the time I saw them first, either would have qualified for inclusion as the DP in the project, since each was steeped in despair. Their relationship, which had been an affectionate and mutually respectful and support-ive one, if never very passionate, had now become hostile and destructive; it was as if, with their circle of relationships stead-ily diminishing, they were clawing at each other and making the other carry the blame and the burden for everything that had become disappointing and frightening.

In the early sessions we focused on Rosa's mourning for her dead brothers and her fear for her own life, and she slowly placed this in a perspective that allowed her to be sad without being panic-stricken. We also established a working relation-ship of affection and respect, in which my liking for them was reciprocated by Rube treating me with old-fashioned gallantry, while Rose called me "Babes". However, their mutual rage, rejection, and recrimination repeatedly erupted. After one particularly horrendous session, in which their destructive battling had again and again overwhelmed their hard-won progress, I found myself overcome with sadness and distress, with a kind of disgust at being a member of the human race, in which lives that had been lived with courage and dignity could be soured and demolished towards the end by a kind of blind panic: my image was of people in a shipwreck stamping on each other's faces in a desperate attempt to reach the lifeboat.

In the next session, I read them the riot act. I made an eloquent speech about my perception of their situation and my own helplessness in the face of their repeated demolition of any-thing good they could hold onto in the relationship. The speech started, "Now, Rose and Rube, I know I'm young enough to be your daughter, but I feel I must say to you . . .". From then on they showed a marked improvement, which continued for a few more sessions and throughout follow-up. They reported themselves much shocked and touched by my speech, and said that on the occasions where they had started to lapse into the destructiveness that now threatened to become a new habit, one or the other would put the brakes on, saying, "Elsa will be so upset with us"! On two-year follow-up, I was touched and pleased to see that they were both well, together—and alive!

Conclusion

Systemic couples therapy for depression—which is the crucial component? Is there something particular about depression that makes it amenable to systemic therapy? Perhaps so: since the time of Job, depression has been available for different constructions of meaning and causation. It may therefore be that a therapeutic approach that holds itself open to multiple meanings is useful in the deconstruction of a phenomenon where the meaning given to the symptoms leads to divergent and serious consequences. The presence of the couple is also probably of significance, in that their cooperation in the business of therapy means that the dilemma is less likely to be categorized as a problem of individual pathology, and changes made in the session are more likely to be stabilized in the everyday lives of the couple and the family. May I be forgiven a bias if I also state that a systemic approach, open to feedback and to constant interrogation of meaning, is likely to prove useful in many diverse difficulties precisely because it assumes that the answers, whatever they are, are likely to be contained in the multiple resources of the client or patient, rather than in the narrow repertoire of the therapist.

CHAPTER FOUR

Working with depression, II

Eia Asen

Background information

Rosie M. is a 31-year-old white working-class woman with 25 years' worth of experiences with psychiatric services. As a 6-year-old child, she was referred by her GP to the local child-guidance clinic because of being "very low, crying all the time, miserable and no friends". She was seen over a period of six months on altogether eight occasions, first with her mother, then by herself, and once with her step-father. Some improvements were reported. At the age of 8, she was re-referred, this time by the school. The teachers reported her to be "low, isolated, without friends". She was assessed and tested by a child psychologist, and this was followed by some school-based work. Rosie also received six sessions of individual counselling. At the age of 10, another referral was made, this time by her parents, because of "depression". Individual child psychotherapy was offered, and after some wait Rosie attended once-weekly for one year. Rosie was 13 when her parents contacted the (re-named) Child and Family Consultation Service. They described her as "depressed and very difficult to manage at home". Family therapy was offered, but Rosie dropped out after the second session. Eight months later she was admitted to the local hospital after taking a paracetamol overdose. The visiting child psychiatrist made the diagnosis of "clinical depression" and put her on antidepressants. Two months later, Rosie took a second overdose, this time using the prescribed medication. The medical response was swift and predictable: Rosie was put on a new brand of antidepressants, and these were meant to be kept by her mother and dispensed each day. Only six weeks later, Rosie had taken another overdose, paracetamol on this occasion, and this led to her being admitted to an adolescent unit. Once there, she had a fairly turbulent time: she started cutting herself and refused to see her parents throughout her stay. Nine months later, now nearly 16, Rosie was discharged. She did not return to school but went to live in a squat. She made dubious friends and started taking drugs. Her medical notes show that she took three further overdoses between the ages of 16 and 18 but that she was not given any specific treatments. She had a six-week in-patient admission at the age of 18, followed by three further in-patient admissions between the ages of 18 and 26. The recorded diagnoses varied from "depressive illness" to "schizoaffective disorder" to "personality disorder". Since then, she had seen different psychiatrists on numerous occasions, with a whole range of antidepressants prescribed.

The referral letter contained a lot of information about her psychiatric "career", but remarkably little about her personal and family history. She was clearly seen by her referrer as a "case". It was mentioned in passing that she had a 7-year-old son, Paul, from a previous relationship and a 1-year-old daughter, Lisa, from her current partner, Jack.

COMMENTARY: Psychiatric work contexts tend to attract psychiatrically framed referrals or "cases" which arrive with specific histories. The therapist needs to respect these framings on the one hand, whilst not getting organized by them on the other. This is easier said than done, given that it is impossible not to have some kind of "heart-sink" feeling and not being particularly optimistic about the prospect of more treatment or therapy in cases such as these. Entertaining a whole range of systemic hypotheses—as described in chapter two—has, therefore, a positively liberating effect: it allows, at least temporarily, to get away from the traditional

understanding of the patient's depression. In the past, such a referral would have brought out some hubris in me, resulting in heroic
efforts to "cure" this person and her family—above all to demonstrate the superiority of the systemic approach. However, after
plenty of sobering experiences over the years, I did not entertain
such rescue fantasies at the point of taking this particular client
and her partner on for therapy. Instead, I thought that my therapeutic efforts would be unlikely to undo a 26-year-long history of
help-seeking behaviours and psychiatric responses. My aims were
consequently much more modest: to introduce some new ways of
thinking about depression and to involve the partner in this exploration, in the hope that this might affect the depressive symptoms.

Session outline

Session 1: Respecting the patient's depression

Jack was the first to speak. He stated that he was "about to
leave Rosie for good because she is always down". He said that he
had not wanted to come to the clinic, as "it's her problem . . . it's
not my fault . . . she has been depressed long before we got together". Rosie confirmed what Jack had said: "I don't think it's fair
on him . . . he has really tried hard . . . I have just got this depression, have had it for years, just don't seem to get rid of it. And now
it causes all our arguments—we would not argue if I was not
depressed." The therapist asked Rosie about her depression, when
it started, how it progressed and so on and ensured that Jack
remained involved in actively listening to Rosie's story of her depression by constantly checking with him ("Is this new to you?
Had you known about this?") and asking Rosie, from time to time:
"When had you told this to Jack first? And what was his response
when you told him about your depression?" This resulted in some
spontaneous discussion between the two of them, with Rosie ac-
cusing Jack of "never" listening to what she said and Jack replying
that she "never" stopped talking about the past. "Only because
you never listen", said Rosie. At this point, Jack became impatient,
got up, and reached for his coat, ready to leave the room. The
therapist thanked Jack for attending together with Rosie and asked

whether he would stay just a few more minutes, as "it is useful to have someone else from the family present to help. We know that if one person is depressed it affects the partner and children—and we also know that their responses affect the person's depression. So it is helpful to hear from you, Jack, what Rosie's depression is like and how you and other people get affected by it." Jack then launched into a self-pitying monologue that was also highly critical of Rosie. The therapist did not interrupt him other than to ask occasionally, "and if she does that . . . what do you do . . . and how does she respond to that". He also brought in Rosie by asking her from time to time to comment on what Jack had said. The therapist did not encourage either of them to discuss directly their different viewpoints and, for the rest of this session, attempted to defuse any emerging conflicts between the two of them. At the end of this first session, the therapist stated that it had been helpful to hear their different perspectives and that there would be more opportunity in the next few sessions for each of them to make clearer their own respective positions. He ended the meeting by stating: "Therefore I recommend that you do not discuss any further what you have talked about here today until the next time we meet."

COMMENTARY: Rosie had been defined—and probably defined herself—as "depressed" and having "patient status". The therapist assumed that not only she but also Jack would have resisted any attempt to make their relationship "the problem". In fact, Jack made endless attempts to reassure the therapist that he was not to blame. Despite being tempted to do so, the therapist deliberately did not challenge the couple's apparent problem definition and focus. As the differences between both became more overt, and particularly when Jack seemed to "test" the therapeutic setting (and implicitly the position of the therapist) by behaving as if he was going to leave, the therapist thought it necessary to temporarily stabilize the situation by confirming their established roles—Rosie being the patient, Jack the "suffering" partner of a depressed patient. It seemed that both felt reassured by the therapist apparently joining them in accepting this "arrangement". The therapist's comment at the end of the session was designed to give a signal that there might be risks if conflicts unearthed in sessions were to spill over into ordinary life.

Session 2: The partner as informant

Jack was again the first to speak. He said that they had not argued at all during the previous week and that Rosie had been "very depressed". Rosie silently nodded her head as Jack continued talking. The therapist invited Jack to say more about Rosie's depression—its origins, fluctuations, his theories about the nature of depression. Jack talked about what he called "the family history of depression" in Rosie's family. He seemed very knowledgeable about her upbringing and listed even some remote members of the extended family and their medical symptoms and diseases. For the first half of the session, Rosie listened almost impassively. The therapist asked her from time to time if she wanted to add anything, and she supplied specific details about her self-harming, admissions to hospitals, and the side-effects and ineffectiveness of all the different antidepressants she had been prescribed. When asked which of Jack's many different theories regarding her depression she found particularly fitting, she said: "It's to do with me and relationships . . . many years ago and now . . . and I don't want my children to grow up like me."

Therapist: "What would have to be different for your children to have a life without depression?"

Rosie: "If my parents had got on, that at least would have been a start . . ."

Therapist: (*cautiously*) "Is that the same or different for your children?"

Jack: "We don't get on well a lot of the time."

Therapist: "And is this because of the depression?"

Jack: "The depression doesn't help. But there is many other things."

Therapist: "Maybe you want to talk about that at some stage, but I want to remember that you are here because of Rosie's depression and I don't want to ask too much about your relationship . . ."

Jack: "I don't mind . . . it may all be linked."

Rosie: "Doctor, do you think my depression is ever going to be cured?"

Jack: "We are not talking about your depression now . . . we are talking about us!"

Therapist: "Well, I will leave it to you how much you want to discuss your relationship when you come here. You both need to let me know when you want to do that and when it's perhaps inappropriate. In the meantime, I suggest that over the course of the next week you, Jack, really watch Rosie's depression. See how it fluctuates, because depression does not stand still, it moves. Perhaps you could keep a diary how it changes from one day to another and record this, and next time we meet we can study the depression more. Maybe you, Rosie, should make your own notes, just perhaps see what makes the depression better and worse. You may even wish to rate it, like giving it a mark . . ."

COMMENTARY: It is only when the couple is ready and gives explicit permission to tackle relationship issues that the therapist will start working with these. In this session, the therapist accepts the position of one of the partners being "the patient who suffers from depression", at least at one level. At another level, he questions using an interactional frame. Behaving as if one saw the partner as an "informant" (informing on the relative, in time-honoured traditional psychiatric fashion) is more likely to be acceptable to the couple at this phase of therapy, and here the therapist is particularly sensitive to feedback. It would appear that Rosie is more reluctant to involve her partner in the problem definition, possibly protecting him. Yet, unlike a traditional psychiatric interview where the "informant" is interviewed separately from the "patient", this context includes both who cannot but respond to what the other says. The focus of the inter-session task is on depression as if it were "externalized", with its fluctuations monitored and the contextual occurrences noted.

Session 3: Graduating from informant to co-worker

Both partners arrived at the session armed with the previous week's depression diaries. The therapist expressed surprise that they both had actually carried out this task, wondering aloud as to whether they had thought that without the "homework" the "headmaster"/therapist would have been cross. This set a somewhat playful tone for this session. The therapist asked Rosie what Jack might have written down, and she speculated. Jack was asked not to give his feedback immediately. Rosie continued imagining how her partner had seen her depression fluctuating over the previous weeks and particularly the times when she imagined he thought that she had been less depressed. The therapist asked: "And if Jack had thought you were less depressed then, would he have got it right or not?" Rosie smiled and replied "no". The therapist asked Jack to respond to what Rosie had said, and they started comparing notes, checking out his assumptions about her depression and her assumptions about how he dealt with what they both termed "depression". Later in the session, the therapist asked Jack whether he himself believed that anything he ever did might have a positive effect on Rosie's mood. He paused and then gave two examples. Rosie quickly added another. The therapist then asked Jack whether there was anything that he could do to make her moods worse—intentionally or unintentionally. Jack paused for quite some time and then replied: "you're not suggesting that I am causing her depression, are you?"

> Therapist: (*turning to Rosie*) "What is your response to Jack's question?"
>
> Rosie: "No, he is not causing it, but there are things that he might not do so that my depression does not get worse . . ."
>
> Therapist: "Do you want to ask Rosie what these are?"
>
> Jack: "I think I know anyway . . ."

Both then started talking about how they were affecting one another, examining the effects of her depression on him and his responses to her symptoms and how these were made better or worse by what he did and did not do.

COMMENTARY: In this session there is a shift from the idea that the depression was only belonging to Rosie, with Jack's involvement being gradually highlighted. The use of hypothetical circular questions helped in opening up this area. When there is such a shift, systemic therapists feel triumphant: therapy seems to be working, and the foundations are laid for viewing depression in context. From here onwards, it would seem that systemic therapy unfolds as it does in most cases, irrespective of what the initial presenting problem was. In this sense, the therapy that follows is not depression-specific.

Session 4: Depression as partnership issue

This time Rosie started the session by describing how her depression had been "up and down" over the previous few weeks and how they had both started talking about how some of this might have something to do with the way he responded to her. Jack said he had identified a number of things he could do to cheer her up. Rosie responded by questioning Jack as to why, if he knew, he was hardly ever doing putting this into practice, and she stated, "I find this very depressing".

Jack: "You find me depressing?"

Rosie: "Yes."

Therapist: "Perhaps you both need to discuss what it is that you each find depressing."

This led them to talk about concrete relationship issues, such as the "typical" arguments they had every Sunday about whether to have a family outing or not, when to visit which in-laws, how much money to spend on which items, and so forth.

Therapist: "If you had to choose one of these issues and discuss how to make things less 'depressing', which one would each of you pick?"

After some discussion they agreed to discuss the following weekend's outing. This soon turned into a major argument, with voices raised. Jack turned to the therapist and stated that Rosie was only arguing because of her depression.

Therapist: (*addressing Rosie*) "Are you depressed right now or are you angry?"

Rosie: "I don't quite know."

Therapist: (*to Jack*) "How do you know when she is upset? How do you know when she is angry or depressed?"

Jack looked puzzled. Rosie said nothing. This led to a very open exploration of how each of them used her "depression" as excuses for not doing anything different.

COMMENTARY: Whilst still making ample use of the word "depressed", it is gradually transformed into a shared concept, denoting not necessarily illness but ways of interacting for both partners. The suggested enactment created tension in the session, resulting in them both addressing concrete relationship issues. Is there anything specific in this session that therapists would only do with couples where there is a depressed partner? My answer is a definite "no": we are now in the business of doing systemic therapy where one person happens to be called "depressed" but where interactional issues become the main focus.

Session 5: Arguments instead of depression talk

Both Rosie and Jack looked miserable. They had had an awful week. The outing had been a total failure, with Jack saying that he had been "too depressed" to face going to the zoo. He added that Rosie had not been particularly depressed—"just very irritable . . . like me . . . sometimes we are just angry". They had argued a lot, over trivial matters. The therapist asked each of them how they were able to differentiate between "being irritable", "being angry", and "being depressed".

Therapist: "What is a typical situation where you think he is angry? How would you know he is not depressed? And how would you know that she is irritable rather than depressed? Would your responses be any different?"

Both partners started examining their own and the other's responses and engaged in a reflective, non-argumentative conversation. The therapist suggested that they might want to keep a diary for the next week and collect and label their own and the other's behaviours in terms of the three categories: "irritation", "anger", and "depression".

COMMENTARY: The gradual deconstruction of the notion of depression had the effect of getting each partner to re-examine familiar behaviours and interactions using a different frame. Much has been written about the relationship between depression and suppressed anger, and there exists a "prejudice"—equally shared by many clients and therapists alike—that if people could only get angry they would be less depressed. I no longer subscribe to this prejudice: what is termed "depression" has very different meanings for the same person in different contexts. It may be temporarily "convenient" for a therapist to label a depressed behaviour as "angry", if only to provoke a person or couple to use a different frame. However, if a therapist actually believes that "depression *is* suppressed anger", then this conviction may lead the therapist to ask the client to *ex-press* the anger—in the hope that the client may therefore get rid of it and be less depressed. This hydraulic model of change does not fit easily into a systemic framework. The systemic therapist's task is to get client and partner to question their habitual ways of seeing things, thus inducing reflection that allows examination of "symptoms" within a whole variety of different contexts—and thus creating a whole string of new meanings that then inform interaction and behaviour.

Session 6: Reframing depression as "convenient strategy"

Rosie and Jack talked about how the process of observation had made them aware that there was "more to life than just depression". Rosie said that, looking back, she was often hiding her rage behind the "comfortable" formula of "I'm very depressed today"—"It just gets me out of difficult situations". Asked by the therapist whether he at times found Rosie's depression "convenient", Jack replied: "I guess, it's an easy option . . . I can then blame this thing called 'depression' which is almost outside Rosie's control . . . I'd find it more difficult to criticize her for the things I don't like about her . . . and I don't think she'd like it." Both then talked about what it was like to be constantly criticized. Rosie spoke about what it had been like for her as a child to have very critical parents—"Nothing I ever did was right."

> Therapist: "Do you think becoming depressed saved you from being criticized?"

> Rosie: "I never thought of it that way . . . I suppose when I got first depressed they were much nicer . . . they treated me as if I was ill . . ."

She acknowledged that this might have been an important dynamic but added: "I think my parents got really fed up with me after a while . . . and then I just couldn't stop getting depressed."

> Jack: "I remember when the two of us first met . . . I just felt you were very vulnerable . . . I didn't dare to say anything to upset you."

> Rosie: (*seemingly shocked*) "You mean you felt controlled by me or what you thought was my depression?"

The rest of the session was spent speculating about the effects of no longer being "allowed" to use depression as a shield—would the "truth" hurt too much? How could they both find ways of being open without being too critical?

COMMENTARY: Here, connections are being made between the "presenting problem" and past issues. Of course, framing depression as a "strategy" rather than an illness could be said to be a strategy in its own right: assigning purpose to what may have been defined as an illness "visiting" a patient (or indeed her brain) is a deliberate new meaning frame, aimed at perturbing the couple's familiar way of seeing things.

Sessions 7–10: Revealing abuse

Jack looked particularly angry when the coupled arrived for the next session: "We've had a terrible week . . . I prefer her depressed."

Jack then talked about how he had started remembering his own childhood, with his parents constantly arguing in front of the children—"my mother always picked on my dad". He said he had then decided that he would never get married—or if he did, then to a woman who would not want to have arguments.

> Therapist: "So, do you think that Rosie's depression is the price you both have to pay for domestic peace?"
>
> Jack: "So-called peace."

The therapist then asked Rosie to find out more about Jack's childhood, his teenage years, and the expectations he had for his new family. Rosie said that they had never talked about this, and Jack replied that Rosie had always wanted to talk about her own background and difficult life. This was reframed by the therapist as a possible protective manoeuvre on Rosie's part—protecting Jack from getting sad about his own life.

At this point the therapist encouraged Rosie to pretend that she was Jack's "counsellor", enabling him to talk about difficulties in his life. Jack resisted at first, but, with his partner's help, bit by bit he revealed a childhood characterized by physical abuse from his father and general emotional neglect from both of his parents. He cried during this and the following two sessions, and he said he was surprised to see Rosie be "so strong and positive".

COMMENTARY: The focus is now on the "non-symptomatic" partner, with the "patient" deliberately placed in the role of "therapist". This was not forced but occurred slowly over quite a number of sessions. Jack showed his vulnerabilities, when the therapeutic context permitted it. Therapy often takes unexpected turns (unexpected to clients and therapists alike), and a person originally defined as "strong", "powerful", or "competent" may during the course of systemic work seem at times to behave in quite opposite ways. Seeing one another differently perturbs seemingly mutually convenient partnership arrangements and may produce tears in unexpected quarters. Is this course of events specific to working with depression? Of course it is not! At this point in the therapeutic process, the presenting problem seems irrelevant. Experienced therapists will have seen such sessions with couples and families presenting with anorexia, anxiety, violence, and abuse.

Session 11: Addressing distance in the couple's relationship

Rosie started this session by saying that "something has happened in my childhood that has made me feel distant". She was unable to say what this "something" was. Jack respected this, and he remarked that there was often "a lot of distance between you and me". They talked about aspects of their sexual relationship and how this had its "ups and downs". Both, somewhat embarrassed, moved away from this topic and started talking about their children. Rosie expressed concerns about how her son might be affected by all this. It was agreed that they would bring him along on the next occasion.

COMMENTARY: In this session, the term "depression" was not mentioned at all by either partner. Issues regarding their sexual relationship were touched upon but not pursued by the therapist as Jack and Rosie both seemed embarrassed. The therapist went along with their decision to bring the son for the next session, possibly as a distance-regulating manoeuvre. What role and place do significant others have in an activity termed "couple therapy"? It is my view that other family members (or other important relationships) are almost always present in sessions even if they are physically absent. At certain stages during therapy, their (physically absent) presence can be so overwhelming that I raise issues about them joining the sessions in the future. This is not a prescription or instruction but is generally introduced as: "What would be the advantages and disadvantages of having person x here next time? Which issues might that help you to address—and which not?" This induces a process of reflection, giving a message that the therapeutic system is "open" (Jenkins & Asen, 1992), so that significant others can join at the invitation of the clients. In about a fifth of the couples I saw during the project, other family members joined for up to two sessions—children, parents, grandparents, and aunts.

Session 12: Mother and son

Jack had decided, in consultation with Rosie, that this session should be "for mother and son only". Paul, who seemed a bright boy, took a seat as far away as possible from his mother. Rosie described how "distant" her son was and that he never wanted to be close to his mother, including sitting on her lap.

Therapist: "When was the last time that you sat on your mum's lap?"

Rosie: "He never wants to sit on my lap."

Paul: "She doesn't want me to."

Rosie: "You never ask me . . ."

Therapist: "What would happen if you asked him to sit on your lap now?"

Paul: "Look at her face . . ."

Therapist: "What does that face tell you?"

Paul: "She doesn't like it."

Rosie: "Do you want to sit on my lap?"

Paul: (*big smile*) "Yes."

At this point, Paul walked over to his mother, hugged her, and sat on her lap. Rosie seemed embarrassed, and over the next fifteen minutes she and her son experimented with a comfortable degree of closeness. Rosie said that she very much experienced her son's wish to be close as overwhelming. She was near to tears. Paul was very much aware of her distress and tried to comfort her. Rosie then asked to see the therapist on her own. She broke down and sobbed uncontrollably for a few minutes. She then talked about Paul being the same age that she was when "it all started". She could or would not say what "it" was. She then spoke about Paul's need for closeness, just the way she had wanted it herself, from her own mother. She talked about how her mother had been unable to be physically and emotionally close to her and how she felt she had never been able to confide in her.

COMMENTARY: In this session Rosie became aware of how the issue of distance in current relationships was connected with her past experiences and re-enacted in the present. Paul helped her to experience this, acting almost as an honorary "co-therapist", enabling his mother to make the first connections between past and present. Clearly there are some potential ethical issues of using a boy to help his mother, and it is the therapist's responsibility to protect Paul from being ab-used in the name of therapy. However, experiencing his mother connecting with him seemed to be a new (or forgotten) emotional event, which, I later discovered, was a first significant step to rebuilding their relationship. Nevertheless, I considered how to use this session to progress the work regarding the couple relationship, hoping that Rosie would feed back to Jack what had happened and that this would produce reverberations or resonances in their relationship.

Session 13: Regulating distance

Rosie started the session by describing how she had told Jack what had happened in the previous meeting with her son.. She had been very moved and she had talked a lot to Jack about how she herself had felt at Paul's age, with her mother being very distant and her step-father making inappropriate physical advances: "I just froze." Feeling her son sitting on her lap created a whole range of mixed feelings: it made her feel "cheap", and yet at the same time it made her feel very close and warm towards her son, wishing to embrace him. She said that she had cried every day over the past fortnight, "but I am not depressed . . . I just feel so sad about what I have not given to my son . . . and what happened to me". Jack and Rosie than spoke about their own relationship, the distance between them, how there could be "safe" closeness, and their fears and hopes for the future of their relationship.

Session 14–15: Connecting past patterns in the present and future

In these sessions, both partners discussed the respective expectations they each had brought into this relationship and how these had been based on their very individual experiences of being brought up in their families of origin. Rosie brought her mother to Session 15 as she felt this might clarify issues from the past: "Maybe I can be a better mother if I understand what my mother went through . . ."

Session 16: Relapse prevention

Thirty weeks into the treatment, the couple asked for a "holiday" from therapy. However, they wanted some reassurance that they could return if necessary. In the event, they made contact two months later, saying that things were fine but that they wanted to think about how a relapse both in Rosie's depression as well as in the quality of their relationship could be prevented. This session took place shortly before the nine-month limit of the permitted length of therapy.

* * *

Rosie did not have any signs and symptoms of depression at the end of therapy nor on the two-year follow-up. In all, there had been sixteen sessions, thirteen of which were with the couple only, one with Rosie, Jack, and both children, one with Rosie and her mother, and one with Rosie and her son.

COMMENTARY: Depression, figuring so prominently in this woman's life, was at the beginning of therapy the presenting patient—to whom Rosie seemed to be attached if not married. The initial therapeutic work was very respectful of this almost lifelong partner named depression. However, during subsequent sessions her other partner, Jack, gradually displaced his rival, with depression being bit by bit deconstructed, to a point when "depression" lost its role in the couple's life. The first few sessions were very depression-specific, but increasingly the therapeutic work resembled very much that of many other couples or families, irrespective of the initial presentation. At a later stage the therapeutic system was widened and other family members attended. The last phase of therapy consisted of "relapse prevention", a term borrowed from work with "ill" patients in medical settings. This actual term was directly used with Rosie and Jack, who seemed to be able to relate to it. It may be appropriate to make use of the term "relapse prevention" when working with persons who have had overexposure to the medical system and who see themselves as being "patients" suffering from recognized "illnesses". This pays due respect to the importance of the illness and its associated symptoms, and how difficult it is to let go of what has become part of one's identity which is constantly being reinforced by the medical system—and the family.

CHAPTER FIVE

Themes and variations

While participating in the study, both during the period of direct work with couples and subsequently when we were given access to the results, we found ourselves struck by a number of themes that seemed of particular significance in working with this client group under these particular circumstances. Some of these themes will, of course, be of general interest in all systemic work, or in all couples work; some are perhaps more relevant to the particular context of this work. We discuss in this chapter the themes that proved of relevance to both of us here; other themes are taken up in the individual clinical chapters (chapters three and four). Some of the themes are clinically significant, while others relate more to the experience, for clinicians, of being researched.

Working on the engagement of partners

Eia Asen

Working in a public context marked as "psychiatric" invites referrals different to those that one would receive in, for example, a
private setting that in its official description contains the word
"Family Therapy", "Systemic Consultation", or such like. This, of
course, very much affects the responses to any such referrals.
Whilst in a public psychiatric setting some of the referrers wish
their patients (this is what they are actually called) to have family
or couple therapy in addition to other forms of treatment, at least
half of these patients turn up for their first appointment by themselves. The reasons for this are manifold: poor preparation for this
type of work by referrers, a wish to retain "patient" status, fears of
subjecting oneself to this unknown "new" therapy, and so forth.
Working in such a setting has taught me to work with whoever
turns up and to respect the power of the "illness", the diagnosis,
and the construction of the presenting person as "patient". This
implies that the therapist should behave as if any other family
member were a potential resource to help the treatment of the
patient—hence the term "partner-assisted" or "family-assisted"
therapy, or, more medically oriented, "treatment". I therefore felt
familiar with the referral process and the problem definitions of
the depressed patients—or, more correctly, individuals diagnosed
by psychiatrists as suffering from clinical depression and individuals who went along with receiving such a label. I knew that a
major part of the initial work had to involve recruiting the partner
and keep him or her in treatment. Hence, almost all of my initial
sessions focused on the symptoms of depression, respecting the
partner as a potential informant and helper—with the result that
none of the partners (and designated patients) dropped out. Use
was made of telephone contact with individuals and their partners
if they had missed appointments.

The research protocol stipulated that the treatment approaches
had to be "pure": patients receiving couple therapy were not permitted to be on medication. GPs were requested to put stickers on
their patients' case notes to ensure that they would not be offered
medication or, if medication was considered necessary, that they
would be removed from the trial. Therapists were also made

aware of this. In the event, none of the patients in the couple group received any form of psychotropic medication.

In ordinary psychotherapy practice, however, clients may well take medication while engaged in therapy. One would maintain an open-minded and neutral position in relation to this whilst inviting the client to speculate about the advantages and disadvantages of remaining on medication or giving it up.

The case history I presented in chapter four is a typical illustration of the work I have done with this group of patients and their partners. I use the unfashionable word "patient" deliberately: the context of the study, the hospital setting, the emphasis and diagnosis and diagnostic procedures—all this made me respect the person who came "with" depression (accompanied by depression) to the first session. The partner was often a reluctant companion, and this meant that one had to move very slowly to construct a setting where the partner became a "partner to the depression". It has to be said that some of the depressed patients presented, from the first session onwards, their relationship as the main reason for their depression, and, if the partner agreed with this, traditional systemic work could start immediately, allowing the therapist to be potentially less respectful in relation to the presenting symptom and its alleged "location".

In this case example, "depression" figured prominently in Rosie's life, a notion reinforced over many years by the medical system. It seemed that she herself had become attached to this notion: it had become part of her identity. In a sense it was Depression that was the presenting patient. It seemed that only by taking this "patient" seriously was it possible to gradually challenge its power, leading to its deconstruction and the construction of the relationship being the "patient" to be worked with. Whilst the first few sessions appeared depression-specific, from Session 4 or 5 onwards the therapeutic work resembled very much that of many couples or families, irrespective of the initial presentation. The term "relapse prevention", borrowed (in view of the context of the research project) from medical settings, may be appropriate in work with medicalized patients, never letting the "illness" or "symptom" out of sight, respecting how difficult it is to let go of what has become part of one's identity, and constantly being reinforced by the medical system—and by the family.

Elsa Jones

I came to this project from a period of about nine years working in a specialist family institute in the voluntary sector, where clients came to us by self-referral. They often did so at the suggestion of other professionals, and many of them presented one family member with a psychiatric or medical/psychosomatic diagnosis. Nevertheless, they were in a "customer" position, in part because we asked fellow professionals to encourage clients to make the referrals themselves. Our practice was to have some discussion or correspondence in order to negotiate attendance at the first session by those whom we considered necessary to address the relevant system, and I followed that practice here. For the most part, both members of the couple attended the first session.

In the case presentation of Kathy and Ken in chapter three, I discussed my approach in a situation where the DP arrived alone for the first session and the partner arrived much later. This is generally a useful way to show enough flexibility to accept what is offered, while nevertheless not risking the even-handedness of future work by allowing oneself to become over-organized by the version presented by one partner in the absence of the other.

> For example, in working with Derek and Dawn, Derek (the DP) arrived alone for the first session, saying that Dawn did intend participating in the therapeutic work but was very angry with him because of a row they had had the night before, and therefore she had wanted him to attend the first session alone—in retrospect, I suspect this was to test his commitment to change. With his agreement, I telephoned her during this first session, in order to start the engagement process, briefly hear her position, and signal my own intention to hear all points of view; the rest of the session was then focused on hearing Derek's account, within the same constraints I discussed in Kathy's case.

Like Eia, I attempt to respect the meaning and weight of the "illness" label, including remaining neutral and open-minded with respect to the use or termination of psychotropic medication. This position derives partly from a systemic interest in the meaning constructions and attributions of clients generally, as well as from the experience of working for many years in psychiatric contexts, where one becomes vividly aware that the discourse around illness, and the participation of many mental (ill-)health professionals, constitute—together with the DP and his or her significant relationships—the relevant system that has to be borne in mind while working, even if it is not possible or desirable to have this whole system in the room (Jones, 1987). As indicated in chapter three, the couples seen in the study varied in the degree to which they presented couple issues as central to the depression, but a majority of them had long-term and significant psychiatric histories. As in all systemic work, it is the therapist's task to understand how the clients construct their lives, with regard to resources and values, as well as with regard to difficulties, so that the resulting work with them will constitute a joint striving towards resolution in terms that make sense to them.

The question of "drop-outs" is discussed later in this chapter.

The social construction of depression

Elsa Jones

As I have said elsewhere (Jones, 1994), "an approach which prides itself on being 'context-minded' cannot continue to ignore the contexts of gender, poverty, inequity and power" in the attempt to find ways of dealing with depression. Current headlines in the newspapers declare that "depression is the West's second biggest killer", and there are advertisements for numerous self-help books. It is likely that many factors contribute to the contextual construction of depression, and to ideas of how to endure or resolve it. Some of these are likely to relate to issues of gender, poverty, racism, abuse, and other constituents of powerlessness; the latter remains for me the most useful way of construing depression.

Gender: Most published findings indicate that more women than men are diagnosed as depressed (for a discussion of some of these studies, see Jones, 1994). It has been speculated that these differences may reside in different life experiences (i.e. women's lives may be more depressing than men's), in different ways of being perceived (i.e. women's distress may be more likely to be read as depression by professionals than men's distress), and in different ways of communicating (i.e. men and women may have learned different ways of signalling their distress). On the one hand, all of these factors seemed relevant in the work with our clients: Derek (see chapter three), for example, said to me in the first session: "They all say I'm depressed, but all I've ever been is angry." By "they", he meant the professionals who had diagnosed him, as well as his partner Dawn; as the work continued it became clear to all of us that Derek was indeed—and with reason—profoundly sad, grieving, and melancholic and had been sorely abused by virtually everyone who had ever been in a position of power in relation to him. However, for Derek, at the start of the therapy, "angry" was the only word he knew for how he felt. The corollary of this, in terms of what the gender discourse does and does not make available to men with regard to their own experiences of being pressed down, is what the partner of a woman DP shouted (in presenting the case for his own depression in contrast to his partner's): "There's no such thing as vulnerable for a man!"

Despite the general validity of the patterns described above, we were surprised to find that our referrals reflected a different picture. Around 40% of the DPs in my group were male. How can we explain this? Perhaps referrers are becoming more sensitive to the sadness and experienced impotence of their male patients? Perhaps men are communicating vulnerability in a more accessible way? It would be interesting to see whether these statistics constitute a fluke of the recruiting process for the project, or whether it heralds a new equity in the context of changing gender relationships, or whether it reflects the "crisis of masculinity" which is now of so much concern to therapists, educators, and society at large.

Poverty: The data for the study show a significant emphasis on the cluster of phenomena that have been widely associated with depression—namely, poverty, unemployment, and occupational class. The combination of limited choice, implied by educational status, and vulnerability to unemployment and poverty can render an individual helpless in the struggle to maintain self-esteem and the sense of being a valuable member of their community. Of the group with whom I worked, nearly 60% lived in poverty; 45% of the DPs and about 40% of their partners were not in work. This does not imply that there are no intra-individual or interpersonal factors in the causation and maintenance of depression; however, it can make a difference to someone's sense of worth and resilience in the face of adversity whether the messages from the wider environment reinforce or contradict a feeling of worthlessness.

Racism: Eighty-seven percent of the DPs in the study were indigenous British whites, a proportion that does not reflect the population figures for London, where the study took place. Twenty-one percent of the DPs I worked with were black or Asian, and in each case it became clear, as we worked, that the experience of discrimination was a more or less significant factor, both generally during their lives and in the course of trying to find help for their depression. Responses to this on the part of the therapist are discussed later in this chapter (see also chapter three).

Abuse: It is known that abuse is seldom reported fully on first enquiry by professionals (Hamberger, 1997b). It is therefore not surprising that a higher prevalence of abuse was reported to the therapists during the course of the sessions than was disclosed to the researchers on initial assessment. In the group with whom I worked, 50% of the DPs had experienced childhood sexual abuse and around 40% reported current violence in the relationship with the partner. Of these, the violence was in all cases a question of the man battering the woman, although in one of these situations the woman also at times acted with generalized violence, such as throwing a brick through a window (see Jacobson & Gottman, 1998). These findings are consistent with general views on the situation of seriously depressed individuals. What was for me the most striking observation was the realization, when I worked out the figures, that 71% of the DPs in my group had been physically abused in childhood (as had over 20% of their partners); many of them also reported witnessing serious violence by one of their parents against the other (see Hughes, 1997; Wolak & Finkelhor, 1998). It is also interesting that the greatest discrepancy between the data as gathered during intake and during therapy occurred here; could it be that clients and mental health professionals now

think it important to note the presence of sexual abuse in childhood, but are not giving the same weight to childhood physical
abuse?

Awareness of these social contexts and influences in the construction and maintenance of our clients' depression meant that at
times it was relevant for the therapist to act in such a way as to
influence the DP's effectiveness in the outside world. In working
with Anne and her partner Andrew (chapter three), I liaised with
the hospital psychiatrist when Anne was admitted after an overdose; subsequently I asked Julian Leff to join us for a session,
partly to tap into his knowledge of the local psychiatric NHS system to help her understand how it worked (and how to "work" it),
and partly to use his clout within that system to help her gain
some sense of choice in how she was dealt with. With other DPs
and their partners, action involved writing back-up letters for re-
housing (e.g. where a battered woman and her partner were attempting to separate) or supporting a DPs increasing political
activism in his housing estate and his desire to inform his neighbours about the links between depression and inner-city poverty.

Eia Asen

Elsa has an ability to formulate ideas that make me at times feel
like a reductionist or somewhat unnecessarily concrete pragmatist.
I tend to defend my limitations by positively connoting this stance
and claiming that I have a special interest in translating predominantly theoretical ideas to clinical practice. In essence I have no
disagreements with Elsa's points and I share her prejudice that
depression is a socially constructed phenomenon. In fact, the findings of this study convince me even more that depression is *not* an
illness. Like Elsa, I believe that a contextual approach needs to
look at the presenting depressed person in a whole variety of different contexts which include not only the couple dynamics, but
also, for example, immediate and extended family relationships,
as well as the social and cultural settings. A close focus on the DP's
depression and the couple relationship maintains a myopic vision,
acceptable perhaps to health managers and politicians who ulti-
mately employ us, but too narrow and one-dimensional to systemic practitioners. Gender, poverty, inequity, and power are all
part of and themselves create specific contexts—albeit at a number

of different logical levels. The multi-contextual stance informs my practice at every stage of the therapeutic encounter, with an awareness of there being many different layers present. Both client(s) and therapist continuously make conscious or non-conscious choices as to which level—or with reference to which context—the encounter is addressing. In my practice, I tend to stick initially to the context of problem definition, as defined by the client(s) and/or referrer. This is what I might arrogantly call the "relevant context". As the (hopefully) therapeutic work unfolds, other contexts will become "relevant", in my client's or indeed my own view; if the latter, references may be made to these "other" contexts. These could include, at one level, references to issues of gender or inequity, or—at another level—to the clients' culture; at yet another level, it may "bring in" the context of the extended family. For example, I might refer to statistics regarding the biased gender distribution of depression and invite the client's reflections about this issue. However, I would quickly move from generalities to specifics, inquiring whether and how this might be an issue for this particular individual or couple in their present life and what the consequences might be. I might bring in other big issues, if appropriate, to do with disability, racism, poverty, or other inequities—which would all provide a context and a frame within which the therapeutic encounter develops. This may result in action outside the consulting-room, which might mean direct action by the therapist in relation to parts of the psychiatric system (as in Elsa's example) or battling with a housing department or actively liaising with a women's refuge to help a client making herself safe.

Elsa reports that in her group of couples a much greater proportion of the DPs than expected turned out to be male (40%), 45% were not in work, and 21% were black or Asian. The characteristics of my sample were somewhat different: approximately 33% male, 15% Asian and Black, and 50% not in work. This apparent difference might be explained by the larger number of clients I saw, probably resulting in a more representative sample being allocated to me via the random allocation process. However, the conclusions drawn from each our representative samples might themselves be an illustration of the process of social construction of depression and thus explain some of the differences in emphasis between Elsa and myself. For example, I did not equate unemployment and poverty—particularly since some of my unemployed clients were far from poor. However, in line with Elsa's thinking, I would consider the impact of unemployment on self-esteem and the sense of being a valuable member in society, and I would raise this at an appropriate point during therapy.

The issue of separation

Eia Asen

The data demonstrated that significantly more couples separated during and after therapy than in the drug-treatment arm of the trial. This was not surprising: at some point during systemic therapy, the relationship is questioned and choices become more apparent. Therapists involved in couple therapy are non-positional in terms of outcome—whether the couple separate or stay together. Almost 25% of my sample separated (including the pilot couples), usually the woman leaving the man. In all of these cases, there was evidence of physical violence between the partners. In another 10%, issues of spouse violence were addressed during sessions, with some reported success. On occasions, individual sessions with the abused spouse were scheduled to discuss ways of keeping safe. There were also sessions with the violent partner to help him find ways of taking responsibility for his actions and to identify ways of protecting the partner from further episodes of violence.

Elsa Jones

In about a third of the couples I saw, separation was not an issue before, during, or after the therapy. Of the remainder, half separated after or during therapy, and the other half resolved their difficulties and remained together in a more committed way than before, in ways that seemed satisfactory to them and to the therapist. Brief examples might illustrate this statement. Following the end of therapy, both Martin and Mary and Kathy and Ken (chapter three) declared a renewed commitment to the relationship: the former moved back together, and the latter got married. On the other hand, John and Jane (not discussed previously) had been prevented from acknowledging the degree to which they had moved apart by Jane's fear that John's depression, following the sudden death of their adolescent daughter some years previously, was such that he would kill himself if she left him. This meant that they were in a mutual trap, where Jane could not leave because John was so depressed, but John could not indicate an end to his depression for fear that Jane would leave. The resulting tangle made both of them feel despairing and disrespectful of themselves and each other. Following the sessions, they were able to separate without the feared dire consequences. The central issue here is for the therapist not to hold a brief for togetherness or separation, but to allow each member of the couple to explore alternatives, consequences, constraints, and potential choices within the freedom of the therapeutic space.

It seems to me that the rate of separation in couples seen by me and by Eia are fairly similar; what does strike me as indicating a difference in our work is the question of couples where violence was a feature of the relationship. Whereas most of these couples in Eia's group separated, most of the ones in my group remained together, and the man (who had in all my cases been the aggressor) was able to stop being violent, while the woman changed her sense of entitlement to safety, and her willingness to protect herself, so that she reacted differently to situations that seemed threatening. I endorse Eia's views about the necessity for separate sessions on occasion, and for a focus first and foremost on safety (see also the discussion in chapter three). I also agree with many of the critics of systemic therapy who advocate that couple therapy should not be done where a woman is being battered by her partner (Jacobson & Gottman, 1998; Kaufman, 1992).

However, I think, as with so much in the area of clinical judgement, that it is often a question of clinical experience and assessment. Like my colleagues in the Ackerman Violence Project (Goldner et al., 1990), I have found that, on the one hand, there are some situations where one would be extremely ill-advised to attempt couple work, and where one's energy and professional authority could best be deployed in trying to steer the woman and the man towards separate therapeutic work and towards safety, even to the point of refusing to work with them otherwise. Lorna and Larry (chapter three) are a case in point. I met with them separately and together; they broke up repeatedly; I focused the work predominantly on questions of safety and responsibility, but I did not refuse to work with them. On the other hand, there are some couples who seem stuck in a potentially dangerous way, but who also seem available for change. These are couples where the woman has felt unable to leave a violent partner, and the man has felt unable to control his violence, and yet the therapist has a sense, while doing the initial exploration with them, that both of them are giving indications of availability for, and strong commitment towards, meaningful change. In these situations, I have usually worked successfully with the couple, where they have been able to change many aspects of the relationship as well as those directly linked to violence. For the most part, this work has involved couple sessions, with very few individual sessions, if any. It is important, in this context, to bear in mind the findings of a wide range of researchers that indicate that "as many as 60% of all married women will be assaulted at some time during the course of their lifetime" (Hamberger, 1997b, pp. 81–82); not all of these relationships will end in separation.

Were I Eia—that is, a male therapist—I think I would experience certain particular difficulties in working in these situations, especially with the use of many individual sessions and with a weighting of the discussion towards separation. I would be concerned at the likelihood of being seen by the man as a challenger and rival, and by the woman as a rescuer and "better man". However, I think Eia's greater willingness to be directive would have been useful to me when I was getting stuck with Lorna and Larry.

Eia Asen

Being a male therapist, I perhaps felt somewhat over-sensitive to not be seen as siding with the violent man. Making continuous references—direct and indirect—to separation as a major option for providing safety away from a violent situation may have had the effect of being perceived as being directive. In fact, with two couples I asked to see the woman on her own to provide her with telephone numbers of women's refuges. This is different from Elsa's practice of providing such information, in that she does this in the presence of the partner.

The therapeutic relationship

Elsa Jones

Systemic therapists have recently been giving more overt attention to the relationship between clients and therapist (Flaskas & Perlesz, 1996; Jones, 1998a). However, we have for a considerably longer time been aware of the implications of power differentials within the therapeutic relationship, particularly along the dimensions of gender, multi-cultural practice, and other potential socially constructed hierarchies of oppression. When working with heterosexual couples, the therapist's gender will coincide with that of one partner and differ from that of the other; this may not signify amongst the other complexities of the relationship, but it may have the effect of making one partner feel outnumbered to a degree that interferes with the cooperative relationship necessary for therapy. We attempted to allow for this by having one female and one male therapist.

However, both of us are white and are likely to be seen as middle class by many clients. The fact that many of the couples in the study were poor or not in work meant that our perceived class and professional status might be significant; in particular situations, our ethnicity or gender might be seen as an obstacle to trust. I have discussed particular ways of approaching such dilemmas in chapter three.

In general, it is important that the therapist should recognize that she or he disposes of greater degrees of power and choice within the therapeutic domain than do her or his clients. Thus, the therapist needs to extend invitations to the clients that may allow them to begin to talk about difficult issues relevant to their lives, in ways that will not further disempower or alarm them. For example, black clients may need to talk about their experiences of racist discrimination, but it will be difficult for them to raise this topic without strong encouragement from therapists who represent—willy-nilly—the establishment and who may also represent the white racist dominant group. Clients who perceive themselves as "one-down" in class terms may not feel able to challenge the therapist's class-based assumptions and values unless the therapist behaves in ways that make this possible.

Eia Asen

One of the key features of the systemic approach is that it offers multiple perspectives: it allows one to view the individual's or couple's issues from many different vantage points; in introducing, sharing, and reflecting with the client(s) on this multiverse, new perspectives hopefully emerge, allowing the clients to take different positions and actions.

Elsa's comments regarding the therapeutic relationship very much resonate with my own thoughts, and I have very little to add. But what about the relationship between the two therapists? Because of time pressure, work load, and geography, the two therapists did not co-work or provide live supervision to each other. This was nothing out of the ordinary as far as my standard practice is concerned: working in a public setting, I rarely have the luxury of co-working cases. During the course of this study, Elsa and I occasionally discussed problematic clinical issues in peer supervision. Again, this seemed a luxury. Generally we just got on with the cases in not-so-splendid isolation.

The context of therapy being done within a research project meant that the therapeutic relationship was much more defined than usual—the protocol permitted up to twenty sessions over a period of up to nine months. Rarely do I work with such time and session "frames" in my ordinary practice. However, it was somewhat interesting to discover at the end of the project that the average number of sessions amounted to twelve, with the average duration of sessions being less than one hour. Is that really very different from what we normally do?

Dealing with the future

The editors noticed that we seemed to place different emphases in our attention to future perspectives near the end of therapy, and so we have been invited to become curious about this.

Eia Asen

The introduction of a strict time frame—as was the case in this study—creates a specific context that affects clinical practice. The arbitrariness of nine months (surely a time frame borrowed from biology), with the possibility of two, ominously termed, "booster" sessions before the two-year follow-up, organized—maybe even medicalized—my thinking. Often therapy, particularly when its frequency and pace is negotiated with clients, is open-ended and needs-led. This clearly has advantages and disadvantages as far as both therapists and clients are concerned. Discussing endings at the beginning of therapy is a very different approach from giving the impression that there is no time limit to therapy and that it could go on "for ever", with the possibility of putting sessions "in the bank". The very specific context of this research project led me to think about the issue of "relapse"—relapsing to what? Well, clearly the depressive symptomatology. Adopting with one part of my brain this medical frame led me to think about the idea of thinking about prevention, not so alien a thought given that much of the EE-reducing psycho-educative family intervention work is preoccupied with preventing relapse by reducing EE in key relatives. As I subscribe to a different model of change, I had little option but to devise different types of relapse-preventing interventions and thus worked with hypothetical scenarios that might signal to the DP or partner that things were going downhill. It was, above all, hypothetical and future questions (Penn, 1985) that were employed in getting couples to identify danger signals and consider ways of responding to these.

Elsa Jones

I do agree with the usefulness of relapse rehearsal, and I would be particularly inclined to do this with clients where the problem (now resolved) had a clear shape and identity, so that one could practice how to see it coming again, avoid it, and so on.

However, I realize that for me there is another meaning to future-related work. This has something to do with the ideas that Peggy Penn (1985) explores in her work on feed-forward questions in relation to imagining the future; it also echoes the interest of Luigi Boscolo and Paolo Bertrando (1993) in the way that the clients' time frame can become frozen in the past or the present, so that a future becomes unimaginable, and it connects with Peter Lang and Elspeth McAdam's ideas about "dreaming conversations" (1997). One of the characteristics of being "stuck" is an inability to move, and specifically to move on in harmony with the flow of change, change which is the only constant. Certain symptoms and events in the lives of families and individuals can particularly have the effect of freezing time: bereavement, the birth of a child whose difficulties signify that it will not grow at the expected rate of development, or certain symptomatic experiences like those diagnosed as schizophrenia and depression. Clients in such a situation will find it difficult to respond to future hypothetical questions, and yet if the therapist can find ways to make such exploration possible, this in itself is likely to act as a trigger for change. Imagining the future means beginning to live it, in the mind, and therefore it begins to become possible.

The experience of being researched

Eia Asen

Has the experience of working with couples affected our clinical work? And if so, how?

Working in a research project is, in part, anxiety provoking. What if it turns out that what one does is less effective than what antidepressant drugs can achieve? It is this dynamic that contributes to the commonly observed phenomenon that therapists in research projects try "extra hard". One of these issues concerns drop-out. Whilst clients not returning for scheduled follow-up sessions may be at times welcome in busy clinics or other settings, it is less welcome when looking at treatment acceptability. Both therapists in this study would immediately get in touch with a couple if they missed a session, so as not to lose any subjects. Once the research data were made public to us, it became evident that none of the couples I had been seeing had dropped out of treatment. This was a somewhat different picture from my general experiences and has since made me question my standard practice. What would happen if I made similar efforts to keep all my clients, at all costs, in treatment? Would my results be better? Which of the clients I saw in the project would have benefited from not being persecuted by a therapist eager to not let go of them? On the other hand, the experience made me question the assumptions we often have when clients do not return for further sessions, believing that they were "better" and therefore no longer required my input.

I think that both Elsa and I share a general scepsis as to what even the most scientific research is able to show—and what it does not show. Both of us were tremendously relieved to discover that what we did seemed to make a difference—measurable by validated research instruments. But what is it that is being measured (Asen et al., 1991)? Doubts remain, above all, as to whether there is such a thing as "systemic couple therapy for depression", clearly a construct itself. Is there anything that is different about the therapy we describe here? Could it not be applied to many other areas of human suffering?

Elsa Jones

Overall, the experience has served to reinforce some of my prejudices and to challenge and change others, while strengthening a feeling that I find hard to describe, but which is made up, I think, of equal parts of duty and subversiveness. Although initially trained rigorously in the language and ethos of research, I have, for some considerable time, positioned myself as one of those psychotherapists who are (rightly) critical of research for not asking the right questions, while (wrongly) not being willing to devote myself to the sort of research I would find appropriate. It seems to me that most traditional researchers resemble the man in the Sufi teaching tale who is discovered searching the ground under a street lamp. Asked what he is doing, he replies that he is searching for his watch, which he has lost. It transpires that he actually lost the watch on another street corner, not the one where he is searching. "So why don't you search there, then?" "Well", he replies, "because the light is better here." On the other hand, it is hard to justify such a lofty critical position when one is not producing better research oneself, and so it seemed to me that I could have the best of both worlds by participating in a well-constructed piece of research as an object of scrutiny rather than a "scrutineer".

What the research data do not show

As a psychologist, trained in the construction and use of research questionnaires and other forms of structured data-collection, I have always been critical of such tools, for two reasons in particular: first, the formality and rigour of questionnaires can obscure the complexity of meanings that the interviewee might experience as best representative of their subjective reality; second, such questionnaires seldom allow for the understanding that the asking of questions brings forth some "realities" while obscuring others. This constructivist position—that we ourselves participate in the creation of the data we attempt to observe—lies at the heart of my systemic psychotherapeutic perspective, and it therefore constitutes a powerful critique of the attempt to map a research grid onto the mountains, valleys, volcanoes, and underground streams of clients' lives and the therapeutic system.

In addition, I take a position—personally and as a psychotherapist—that assumes that life may at times contain tragic and problematic elements that cannot be excised by magic pills or reconstructed narratives. Thus, one may have the view that psychotherapy has contributed to a significant change in someone's life, without believing that this person now has a sufficiently cheerful outlook on life to obtain a low score on the BDI. My work with Derek and Dawn (see also chapter three) is an example of this.

Derek's mother fled from his father's violence before Derek, the youngest of nine children, reached the age of 2 years. He has no certain memory of ever having seen her. His father behaved in a volatile and cruel way towards all the children, and Derek told me and Dawn about many examples of extreme terror throughout his childhood, which included the erection of a flogging scaffold in the backyard where, for example, a brother was left hanging for four days. Before the age of 8, Derek had seen one brother killed by a lynch mob and knew that another brother had been killed in police custody in Britain. His childhood was haunted by the ghosts of his dead brothers; he never told anyone about this because, simply, he knew no one who might respond to this information in a way that might help him. The brutality at home, and the racist discrimination at school, were such that he left school as soon as he was able, having absorbed very little in the way of formal education. Two of his siblings had been diagnosed as schizophrenic, as had his son from a previous marriage (see Bennett & Dennis, in press, regarding the role of racism in the over-diagnosis of schizophrenia amongst black British people). Derek had taken on the task of being the care-taker for everyone in his extended family, so that he was the one called out when a crisis occurred. The fact that all his older siblings looked to him for support did not increase his self-esteem; rather, he felt like a failure because he could not alter their difficult lives sufficiently. Shortly before the start of therapy, Derek had spent three days in police custody and been bound over in court in relation to a serious assault on Dawn and her young son from a previous relationship.

The details above constitute a small sample of the circumstances of Derek's life to that point; as stated in chapter three, he told me, in the first session, that he did not understand his diagnosis of depression, since all he had ever felt was anger. By the end of our work together, Derek showed some small improvement on some of the assessment categories, and by two-year follow-up he had either remained static or slipped back in the direction of his pre-intake status. I think that it would probably be true to say that he remained a man given to melancholia, with a low expectation of life's bounty. However, it seems to me also important to contrast the hard data of the research findings with the soft data of communication during and after therapy. Patients were entitled to a few follow-up sessions where necessary, and, although we did not meet, Derek and Dawn opted to use this entitlement by telephoning me once a year at Christmas time for three years, so that I also received informal anecdotal follow-up. I will give one brief anecdote here in the hope that it may illustrate something about the qualitative changes that Derek made.

Dawn had reported in a session about halfway through the course of therapy that she was angry with Derek because, when she had been confiding something sorrowful to him, he had not stayed focused on her experience but had instead countered with an account of a similar experience he had once had. In response to Dawn's complaint in the session, Derek did not "get the hump" as was his wont, but persisted with the discussion until it became clear that he had meant the offer of a matching experience as a way to indicate empathy, whereas Dawn had felt that it negated her own entitlement to be heard. At this point, he leant over, put his hand on her leg, and said softly and with some placatory laughter: "Give me time, love, I'm still learning." I was struck by the enormous contrast with the angry, inarticulate man of the first session, who knew no expression for his emotions other than anger.

By the end of therapy, many qualitative changes had come about for Derek and Dawn as individuals, as a couple, as parents, and as members of an intricate relationship network. Derek had attended a training course intended, in the first place, to improve his literacy and later to teach him business skills, with a view to self-employment. When they called me for the third annual Christmas call, they reported that Derek's business was running well, that their young daughter and Dawn's young son were both doing extremely well at school, and that Dawn, no longer inhibited by Derek's perceived educational inferiority, had applied for and got a management position in her work. As she said: "You need to take these things into account just to show that we know change goes right through the system."

I am not surprised that, despite these positive factors, Derek should still come across as gloomy and pessimistic on assessment. He carries what a client in another context once called "the burden of knowledge": that is, like others who have experienced some of the horrors that human beings are capable of inflicting on one another, he has looked into "the heart of darkness". Despite this, he finds a way to live his life in such a way that he fulfils Freud's criteria for mental health—that is, he is capable of loving and working.

What the research data do show

An unexpected consequence of the revelation of the final data was, for me, a renewal of my faith in the effectiveness of systemic work, which has sometimes been called brief long therapy. Many of the patients in the study had long psychiatric histories, or suffered from a multitude of contextual and individual handicaps. At the conclusion of each piece of therapy, the therapists completed a questionnaire in which one question asked what we would have done differently if these patients were not being seen in the research context. I found myself quite often saying that I would have seen them for longer. By this, I did not necessarily mean that I would have wanted to increase the number of sessions. In fact, my experience was that where I continued for the full twenty sessions, this was an indication of stuckness rather than of good practice. What I would have liked was to offer occasional sessions (sometimes called "MOT" sessions) to help support the changes that had been made, and to do so over a period of years. There was some provision for this in the short term within the research protocol, if not in the long term, but I was rarely able to make use of it, given that I was based in a different city and therefore less flexible in my availability.

I doubted that some of the patients, given the obstacles in their day-to-day lives, would be able to sustain the changes they had made. For example, at the end of the work with Kathy and Ken (we had done 12 sessions but had come to the end of the time provision) I felt very positive about the changes they had made together, and about the marked changes in Kathy, but I was more concerned about Ken and about the possible effect of a relapse on his part on Kathy's new-found sense of well-being. These concerns were shared by the couple. We all felt that Ken was in a rather newly fledged state, and that there was a risk that he might backslide without the support of the therapy meetings. Should this happen, the knock-on effect on Kathy, and the stress in their relationship, might tumble both of them back into their pre-therapy states of mind. We discussed this thoroughly during the last few sessions and made plans not only to guard against relapse, but also to enable Ken to plan ways of continuing the journey started in the sessions, with Kathy's help and on his own.

I was delighted to see, when I finally gained access to the two-year follow-up results, that they, like many other patients, had not only sustained the changes made by the end of therapy, but had also continued to develop. The BDI chart (Figure 1.1) gives the flavour of this continuous change. In retrospect, my surprise at this finding is probably one of the effects of participation in a research project and the concomitant self-doubt (see below), since the way in which we do systemic therapy is precisely intended to allow clients to have a sense of ownership and competence in relation to the changes they make, so that we can assume that a great deal of the work of therapy is done in the spaces of time outside of the therapy sessions. Having this article of faith reinforced by research data constituted for me an unexpected bonus.

What the data exclude

I was startled to find, when given access to the completed statistical data, that two of my unambiguous successes were being counted as drop-outs from treatment, because they completed the work in, respectively, two and four sessions. Thus my strong advice to systemic therapists participating in research projects would be: read the small print! I had come from a context of work where we regarded an average of about four sessions as normal, and so I was not surprised, in these two cases, that the couple and I should have decided that the work had been satisfactorily completed after just a few sessions. I was aware that we had been set an upper limit for the number of sessions to be done, but I had not taken on board the idea that there had to be a lower limit of six sessions (can I blame this inattention on my ambivalence about participating in the research at all?) My subsequent complaints to the researchers fell on deaf ears; they knew that these were successes, as clearly demonstrated in the follow-up results, but they felt that omitting these from the calculations did not make a difference statistically.

If I had been aware of the lower limit, would I have found a way to persuade the couple to remain in therapy a little longer for the sake of the research? And would this have been ethical? It is, of course, hard to speak with certainty in retrospect. In the two-session case, I think I would not have tried to keep them: one of the reasons why a quick resolution was achieved had to do with the very negative meaning they attributed to being in a psychological therapy; thus, any attempt to hang onto them would likely have given them the impression that I thought that there was something psychiatrically amiss with them. In the other case (see Salman and Safia in chapter three) we could perhaps have continued for two more sessions without negative consequences. They felt, by this time, affectionate towards me and had negotiated, rather shyly, permission for Safia to telephone me on rare occasions as a mother-substitute to talk about her pregnancy; one of the previous sources of tension between the two of them had been the expensive calls Safia, in her loneliness and misery, had made to her mother in her far-distant home. However, it was difficult for them to attend therapy: Salman worked long and unsociable hours, and they lived far from either of the therapy centres, found the cost of travel difficult, and were too proud to accept payment of their fares. Thus, persuading them to come and see me would have imposed hardship on them for my sake, whereas the two or three telephone calls were manageable and happened at their instigation. The birth of a baby girl is, by the way, about as concrete as one might wish to get in the search for outcome indicators, given the nature of the presenting problem!

Being researched

We knew from the beginning that we would feel pressurized by the constraints and scrutiny of the research process, and we tried to defend ourselves against this by repeatedly reminding each other that we could exercise choice when necessary. Built into the research structure was an agreement that patient welfare would override research demands, so that we could, in theory, feel free to act clinically even if this had the effect of removing patients from the research. The effect of this was more psychological than actual and, as I have discussed in chapter three, did not always work.

Despite our best efforts, I was aware at times of being caught up in a competitive ethos in which we as systemic therapists were pitted against "the others", and where we were also pitted against each other. One might adopt a lofty curiosity in which any findings will add to the sum of knowledge, but the fear of being exposed, in public, as a terrible therapist is hard to ignore. Systemic therapists are accustomed to transparency of practice. All trainee family therapists work in front of the one-way screen; many systemic therapists also work regularly under the gaze of our peers. Nevertheless, I found this to be significantly different from the imagined scrutiny of others, who did not share one's theory, or clinical perspective, and whose brief was not to be there as part of the shared therapeutic endeavour, but to observe from a detached "objective" stance. Thinking about the potential influence of this scrutiny on my practice is a bit like trying to answer one of those standard philosophy questions about the reality or otherwise of the fall of an unobserved tree in the forest: how different was my researched practice from my "usual" practice? Certainly self-doubt, and self-consciousness, were more present than usual.

Eia and I did not meet often for peer consultation; when we did, we found that, because of our different orientations and histories, consultation or supervision meant different things to us. This further fuelled my uneasiness about the comparisons between our work that would emerge from the study. As will be obvious from this book, I tend to be discursive and verbose, with a liking for meta-contextual theorizing. I was also accustomed to Milan-style team consultation in which free association and orgies of lineal hypothesizing help me to focus my thinking. I was unable to invite Eia to participate in such meandering discourse, and my experience of his style as much more focused and direct strengthened my assumption that his way of working was likely to be far more appropriate to the client group and the context. Thus, not only did public humiliation await me, it would also stain my particular systemic model! Eia's statements that he harboured similar fears did not convince or reassure me.

I also found many of the pragmatic details of the work uncongenial and not to be recommended for good practice. This may have been due to my idiosyncratic circumstances, where I travelled a long distance to do the work. In consequence, I was not as flexible as I like to be about the spacing of sessions, nor as able to influence the comfort and containment of the setting. I worked in two different venues, on opposite sides of London, necessitating exhausting and unreliable travel between them on public transport. One of the venues is dedicated to therapeutic work, and acted as a supportive home to me and to patients; the other is predominantly used for academic purposes and was less suitable. My colleagues in the systemic and other arms of the project were free to see patients in their own settings; I sometimes found myself alone in a dark building, late at night, discussing violent topics— and once found myself, on the completion of a safety agreement with a couple, locked into the building by the departing cleaners! I would advise others contemplating participation in research projects to consider the importance of having some control over their environment, since my inability to do so was the one most consistently negative influence on my work. If I take seriously the idea that the "self" of the therapist is significantly part of the therapeutic system, then the comfort and sense of containment and safety of the therapist, especially when working with volatile situations, is a necessary constituent of a healing environment.

At the end of it all, I am left with the awareness that, despite the constraints and pressures of the research context, despite the paucity of choice offered to the patients, despite the problems of applying lineal structures to the multiverse of therapeutic discourse, we have—patients, therapists, researchers—shared an important and valuable experience. Perhaps the explanation lies in Dr Johnson's dictum (paraphrased) that the knowledge that one is to be hanged in a fortnight concentrates the mind wonderfully.

And so, finally, to the matter of duty and subversion. I realized, as the research project slowly progressed, and while we all waited for the follow-up results, that the findings were going to be highly significant for systemic therapists working under increasing constraint in the health services, where "evidence-based practice", financial stringency, and a reversion to more traditional biologically based psychiatry are increasingly threatening the survival of systemic psychotherapeutic approaches. I felt it, then, to be a duty to write up this work so as to offer some small support to beleaguered colleagues: it cannot be said too often or too clearly that the work we did does not constitute a new form of psychotherapy, but is systemic therapy with couples, capable of being carried out by all and any of us trained in this way of working. As to subversion, I also became aware, once the results became public, of the enormous power of the dominant discourse of traditional medical opinion, which has not welcomed this signal challenge to the hegemony of drugs treatments, and which has astonished me with the evidence of the subtlety and pervasiveness of its capacity to marginalize and silence dissidence and news of difference. To that degree, then, it has also been a delight to be able to bear witness to the efficacy of a talking cure—and of the resourcefulness of depressed people when given half a chance to empower themselves and to speak in their own voices.

Finale

One of the questions asked repeatedly is whether the results of the London Depression Intervention Trial should be attributed to the specific characteristics of the patients, to those of the therapists, or to those of the psychotherapeutic model. In other words: are the findings generalizable and replicable? Would different systemic therapists have produced different results? How much has to be attributed to the therapist factor? Are patients recruited to a research project different from those who would normally benefit from such an approach?

• *Can the findings be replicated?*

The question of whether or not the findings can be replicated is a very important one, and the answer will profoundly affect future work with depressed patients. We are pleased that various attempts to replicate the findings of the study are in train in quite different contexts. For example, a group of systemic psychotherapists together with research psychiatrists and psychologists in the Netherlands aims to reproduce the original design of the study, using experienced therapists in all three treatment modalities. Another study is under way in the United Kingdom which aims to examine whether less experienced systemic counsellors, working in primary care settings, can be trained and supervised in such work to produce similar outcomes.

- ### *How much is attributable to therapist factors?*

Of course, the question of how much is attributable to therapist factors must be asked. As will be obvious from this book, the two of us are in some ways quite similar and, perhaps significantly, different in others. However, we both have long experience of working as psychotherapists in a wide range of contexts. Observers must therefore be expected to ask whether the outcomes in this study are specific to ourselves or whether they can be replicated by other therapists using the same model. While not dismissing the relevance of individual therapist factors, we do think that the systemic model is the central element accounting for the results. We have stated repeatedly in the book that what was being researched was not a new model of psychotherapy, but the application of systemic therapy to couples where one partner was diagnosed as suffering from significant depression, and where the entire process was subjected to research scrutiny.

We are aware that the findings from this and future studies will have important implications for systemic therapists working in contexts where a changing ethos and economic stringency are requiring therapists to conform to the demands of "evidence-based medicine" which is defined by Sackett et al. (1996) as "the conscientious, explicit and judicious use of current best evidence in making decisions about the care of individual patients" (p. 71).

- ### *How representative are these patients?*

As we discussed in chapter one, the recruitment process may have had the effect of selecting patients at the more severe end of the spectrum. In general work in public settings, the range of presentation is likely to be much wider and will therefore include less seriously depressed clients. Over the years, systemic therapy has been found by its practitioners to be applicable to a very wide range of settings and presenting problems. This study has indicated that systemic therapy can produce good results with seriously and chronically depressed patients; it is therefore logical to assume that it might be even more successful with the everyday range of clients available for this way of working.

- *What do we make of our experiences of working in this research trial?*

As a result of our participation in this project, we find ourselves with a new friendliness towards research, a sense that it is possible to manage the tension of living with simultaneous lineal/circular epistemologies, in the service of making a viable case for our kind of work in the hurly-burly of economic scrutiny. We are aware that managers charged with commissioning services may not have an insider's understanding of the complexities of psychotherapy and may therefore find themselves persuaded by research evidence that has often been based on very small samples and poor and narrow examination of results, leading to major claims regarding the efficacy of specific treatments. If we as systemic therapists want our approach to be valued and funded within the public services, we have to make our work available for evaluation.

Participation in this project has affirmed our perception of the complex interweaving of contexts—social, political, economic, cultural, gender, class, individual, interactional—that shape the experience labelled as "depression". The finding that positive change could occur and be sustained as a consequence of relatively few therapy sessions confirms our belief that systemic therapy is a parsimonious and elegant way to take account of this complexity without having to extend therapy unduly.

So it would seem that this book is not the end of this project, hardly a Finale, but the Overture to other new exciting work in the systemic field.

REFERENCES

Andersen, Tom (1987). Reflecting teams: dialogue and meta-dialogue in clinical work. *Family Process, 26* (4): 415–428.

Asen, Eia (1997). From Milan to Milan: true tales about the structural Milan approach. *Human Systems, 8*: 39–42.

Asen, Karl Eia; Berkowitz, Ruth; Cooklin, Alan; Leff, Julian; Piper, Robin; & Rein, Lorian (1991). Family therapy outcome research: a trial for families, therapists and researchers. *Family Process, 30*: 3–20.

Bateson, Gregory (1972). *Steps to an Ecology of Mind: Collected Essays in Anthropology, Psychiatry, Evolution and Epistemology.* London: Chandler.

Bennett, Elizabeth, & Dennis, Maxine (in press). Adult mental health module. In: Elizabeth Bennett, Maxine Dennis, Nneelam Dosanjh, Aruna Mahtani, Ann Miller, Zenobia Nadirshaw, & Nemisha Patel (Eds.), *Clinical Psychology, "Race" and Culture: A Resource Pack for Trainers.* Leicester: BPS Books.

Bograd, Michele (1999). Strengthening domestic violence theories: intersections of race, class, sexual orientation and gender. *Journal of Marital and Family Therapy, 25* (3): 275–289.

Boscolo, Luigi, & Bertrando, Paolo (1993). *The Times of Time: A New*

Perspective in Systemic Therapy and Consultation. New York: W. W. Norton.

Boscolo, Luigi; Cecchin, Gianfranco; Hoffman, Lynn; & Penn, Peggy (1987). *Milan Systemic Family Therapy: Theoretical and Practical Aspects*. New York: Harper & Row.

Burnham, John B. (1986). *Family Therapy: First Steps towards a Systemic Approach*. London: Tavistock Publications.

Campbell, David; & Draper, Ros (Eds.) (1985). *Applications of Systemic Family Therapy: The Milan Approach*. London: Grune & Stratton.

Context (1999). Sowing the seeds of cultural competence: family therapy training for a multi-ethnic society. The report of the CONFETTI working party on "race", ethnicity and culture in family therapy training. *Context: A Magazine for Family Therapy and Systemic Practice, 44*.

de Shazer, Steve (1985). *Keys to Solution in Brief Therapy*. New York: W. W. Norton.

Dobash, R. Emerson, & Dobash, Russell P. (1992). *Women, Violence and Social Change*. London: Routledge.

Flaskas, Carmel, & Perlesz, Amaryll (Eds.) (1996). *The Therapeutic Relationship in Systemic Therapy*. London: Karnac Books.

Frosh, Stephen (1992). Masculine ideology and psychological therapy. In: Jane M. Ussher & Paula Nicolson (Eds.), *Gender Issues in Clinical Psychology*. London: Routledge.

Geddes, Michael, & Medway, Joan (1977). The symbolic drawing of the family life space. *Family Process, 16*: 219–228.

Geffner, Robert (Ed.) (1997). *Journal of Aggression, Maltreatment and Trauma* (Special Issue), *1* (1).

Goldner, Virginia (1985). Warning: family therapy may be hazardous to your health. *Family Therapy Networker, 9* (6): 19–23.

Goldner, Virginia (1998). The treatment of violence and victimization in intimate relationships. *Family Process, 37* (3): 263–286.

Goldner, Virginia ; Penn, Peggy; Sheinberg, Marcia; & Walker, Gillian (1990). Love and violence: gender paradoxes in volatile attachments. *Family Process, 29* (4): 343–364.

Hamberger, L. Kevin (1997a). Female offenders in domestic violence: a look at actions in their context. *Journal of Aggression, Maltreatment and Trauma, 1* (1): 117–129.

Hamberger, L. Kevin (1997b). Research concerning wife abuse: implications for physician training. *Journal of Aggression, Maltreatment & Trauma, 1* (1): 81–96.

Hare-Mustin, Rachel T. (1998). Challenging traditional discourse in psychotherapy: creating space for alternatives. *Journal of Feminist Family Therapy, 10* (3): 39–56.

Haley, Jay (1976). *Problem-Solving Therapy.* San Francisco, CA: Jossey-Bass.

Hughes, Honore M. (1997). Research concerning children of battered women: clinical implications. In: Robert Geffner (Ed.), *Journal of Aggression, Maltreatment & Trauma, 1* (1): 225–244.

Jacobson, Neil S., & Gottman, John M. (1998). *When Men Batter Women: New Insights into Ending Abusive Relationships.* New York: Simon & Shuster.

Jasinski, Jana L., & Williams, Linda M. (Eds.) (1998). *Partner Violence: A Comprehensive Review of 20 Years of Research.* Thousand Oaks, CA: Sage Publications.

Jenkins, Hugh, & Asen, Karl Eia (1992). Family therapy without the family: a framework for systemic practice. *Journal of Family Therapy, 14:* 1–14.

Jones, Elsa (1987). Brief systemic work in psychiatric settings where a family member has been diagnosed as schizophrenic. *Journal of Family Therapy, 9:* 3–25.

Jones, Elsa (1993). *Family Systems Therapy: Developments in the Milan Systemic Therapies.* Chichester: John Wiley.

Jones, Elsa (1994). Gender and poverty as contexts for depression. *Human Systems: The Journal of Systemic Consultation and Management, 5:* 169–183.

Jones, Elsa (1996). The gender of the therapist as contribution to the construction of meaning in therapy. *Human Systems: The Journal of Systemic Consultation & Management. 7* (4): 237–245. [First published in Maurizio Andolfi, Claudio Angelo, & Marcella De Nichilo (Eds.), *Sentimenti e Sistemi.* Milan: Cortina, 1996.].

Jones, Elsa (1998a). Working with the "self" of the therapist. *Context, 40:* 2–6.

Jones, Elsa (1998b). A feminist systemic therapy? In: Bruna I. Seu & M. Colleen Heenan (Eds.), *Feminism and Psychotherapy: Reflections on Contemporary Theories and Practices.* London: Sage Publications.

Kaufman, Gus Jr (1992). The mysterious disappearance of battered women in family therapists' offices: male privilege colluding with male violence. *Journal of Marital and Family Therapy, 18:* 233–245.

Knudson-Martin, Carmen (1997). The politics of gender in family therapy. *Journal of Marital and Family Therapy, 23* (4): 421–437.

Kuipers, Elisabeth; Leff, Julian; & Lam, Dominic (1992). *Family Work for Schizophrenia: A Practical Guide.* London: Gaskell.

Lang, Peter, & McAdam, Elspeth (1997). Narrative-ating: future dreams in present living. *Human Systems: The Journal of Systemic Consultation and Management, 8* (1): 3–12.

Leff, Julian; Kuipers, Elisabeth; Berkowitz, Ruth; Eberleinfries, Rose-marie; & Sturgeon, David (1982). A controlled trial of social intervention in schizophrenic families. *British Journal of Psychiatry, 141*: 121–134.

Leff, Julian; Vearnals, Simon; Brewin, Chris; Wolff, Geoffrey; Alexander, Barabara; Asen, Eia; Dayson, David; Jones, Elsa; Chisholm, Daniel; & Everitt, Brian (in press). The London Depression Intervention Trial: an RCT of antidepressants versus couple therapy in the treatment and maintenance of depressed people with a partner: clinical outcomes and costs. *British Journal of Psychiatry.*

Maturana, Humberto R., & Varela, Francisco J. (1988). *The Tree of Knowledge: The Biological Roots of Human Understanding.* Boston, MA: Shambala.

McGoldrick, Monica, & Gerson, R. (1985). *Genograms in Family Assessments.* New York & London: W. W. Norton.

Miller, Ann, & Thomas, Lennox (1994). Introducing ideas about racism and culture into family therapy training. *Context. 20*: 25–29.

Minuchin, Salvador (1974). *Families and Family Therapy.* London: Tavistock.

Minuchin, Salvador, & Fishman, H. Charles (1981). *Family Therapy Techniques.* Cambridge, MA: Harvard University Press.

Papp, Peggy (1984). The creative leap: the links between clinical and artistic creativity. *Family Therapy Networker* (September/October): 20–28.

Penn, Peggy (1985). Feed-forward: future questions, future maps. *Family Process, 24*: 299–310.

Perelberg, Rosine Jozef, & Miller, Ann C. (Eds.) (1990). *Gender and Power in Families.* London: Routledge.

Pote, Helen; Stratton, Peter; Cottrell, David; Boston, Paula; Shapiro, David; & Hanks, Helga (1999). *Systemic Family Therapy Manual.* Leeds: University of Leeds.

Reimers, Sigurd, & Dimmock, Brian (1990). Mankind and kind men: an agenda for male family therapists. *Journal of Family Therapy, 12* (2): 167–181.

Sackett, David. L.; Rosenberg, Williams M. C.; Gray, J. A. Muir; Haynes, R. Brian; & Richardson, W. Scott (1996). Evidence-based medicine: what it is and what it isn't. *British Medical Journal, 312*: 71–72.

Schwarzenbach, Felix, & Leff, Julian (1995). "Treatment Integrity of Couple, Cognitive and Drug Therapy for Depression." Unpublished manuscript, Institute of Psychiatry, London.

Selvini Palazzoli, Mara; Boscolo, Luigi; Cecchin, Gianfranco; & Prata, Giuliana (1977). Family rituals: a powerful tool in family therapy. *Family Process, 16*: 445–453.

Selvini Palazzoli, Mara; Boscolo, Luigi; Cecchin, Gianfranco; & Prata, Giuliana (1978). *Paradox and Counterparadox: A New Model in the Therapy of the Family in Schizophrenic Transaction.* New York: Jason Aronson .

Selvini Palazzoli, Mara; Boscolo, Luigi; Cecchin, Gianfranco; & Prata, Giuliana (1980a). Hypothesizing–circularity–neutrality: three guidelines for the conductor of the session. *Family Process, 19*: 3–12.

Selvini Palazzoli, Mara; Boscolo, Luigi; Cecchin, Gianfranco; & Prata, Giuliana (1980b). A ritualised prescription in family therapy: odd days and even days. *Journal of Marital and Family Therapy, 6*: 3–9.

Taffel, Ronald (1991). Why is Daddy so grumpy? In: Thelma Jean Goodrich (Ed.), *Women and Power: Perspectives for Family Therapy.* New York: W. W. Norton.

Tomm, Karl (1987). Interventive interviewing, Part II: reflexive questioning as a means to enable self-healing. *Family Process, 26*: 167–183.

Tomm, Karl (1988). Interventive interviewing, Part III: intending to ask lineal, circular, strategic and reflexive questions. *Family Process, 27*: 1–15.

UKCP (1999). *Training Standards of the Family, Couple, Sexual and Systemic Therapy Section of the United Kingdom Council for Psychotherapy.* London.

Ussher, Jane M., & Nicolson, Paula (Eds.) (1992). *Gender Issues in Clinical Psychology.* London: Routledge.

Vaughn, Christine; & Leff, Julian (1976). The measurement of expressed emotion in the families of psychiatric patients. *British Journal of Social and Clinical Psychology, 15*: 157–165.

Watzlawick, Paul; Weakland, John; & Fisch, Richard (1974). *Change: Principles of Problem Formation and Problem Resolution.* New York: W.W. Norton.

Wolak, Janis, & Finkelhor, David (1998). Children exposed to partner violence. In Jana L. Jasinski & Linda M. Williams (Eds.), *Partner Violence: A Comprehensive Review of 20 Years of Research.* Thousand Oaks, CA: Sage Publications.

INDEX

128

Maturana, Humberto R., 36
McAdam, Elspeth, 107
McGoldrick, Monica, 37
meanings:
    of depression, 24
    and patterns, intergenerational,
        19–20
Medway, Joan, 37
Milan-oriented therapy, 23, 116
Miller, Ann C., 14, 69
Minuchin, Salvador, 27, 31, 32, 33,
    35, 36, 39

neutrality, 17, 18, 27–28
    and discussing issue of
        separation, 44
Nicolson, Paula, 42
non-couple sessions, 43–44
non-judgemental listening, 28

other, seeing oneself through the
    eyes of, 30
outcomes, 110–114. *See also* ending;
    future

Papp, Peggy, 33, 34
partners:
    cause and response to depression,
        16–17
    engagement of, 94–97
    role in therapy, 28
    see also family context
patients:
    selection for research, 120–121
    status, 94, 95
patterns:
    case study, 56–58, 67–68
    and meanings, intergenerational,
        19–20
    past, present. and future (case
        study), 91
Penn, Peggy, 14, 42, 107
    and feed-forward questions, 30
Perelberg, Rosine Jozef, 14
Perlesz, Amaryll, 105
perturbation, as one consequence of
    circular questioning, 36–37

pharmacotherapy, 4. *See also*
    antidepressant medication
physical abuse, and sexual abuse,
    100
positive connotation, 39
positives, focusing on, 34, 40–41
Pote, Helen, 2
poverty, social context of depression,
    98–99, 102
power:
    and therapeutic relationship, 105
    within relationships, 43
    see also empowerment
powerlessness, experience of and
    depression, 46, 67
Prata, Giuliana, 22, 23, 39
presenting symptoms:
    attitude towards, 95
    relevant context, 101
pretend techniques, 40. *See also* "as-
    if"; hypothesizing
problem solving, 34–35

racism:
    and schizophrenia, 111
    social context of depression, 99,
        101
referral:
    reasons for, 17
    process, 94
reframing, 33, 38–39
    case study, 62, 68
    depression as convenient strategy
        (case study), 86–87
Reimers, Sigurd, 59
relapse, 107
    prevention of, 95
    case study, 92
    see also future; outcomes
relevant context, 101
repeating triangles, 56
repetition, as means of confirmation
    28
research project:
    experience as object of, 108–109,
        115–118
    findings, 119–121